MOMS DON'T HAVE TIME TO HAVE KIDS

MOMS DON'T HAVE TIME TO HAVE KIDS

A TIMELESS ANTHOLOGY

Edited by ZIBBY OWENS

Skyhorse Publishing

Skyhorse Publishing books may be purchased in bulk at special discounts for sales promotion, corporate gifts, fund-raising, or educational purposes. Special editions can also be created to specifications. For details, contact the Special Sales Department, Skyhorse Publishing, 307 West 36th Street, 11th Floor, New York, NY 10018 or info@skyhorsepublishing.com.

Visit our website at www.skyhorsepublishing.com.

10 9 8 7 6 5 4 3 2 1

Library of Congress Cataloging-in-Publication Data is available on file.

Cover design by Jovelyn Valle
Cover photo by Kyle Owens

Print ISBN: 978-1-5107-6639-6
Ebook ISBN: 978-1-5107-6640-2

Printed in the United States of America

To my four kids who I will ALWAYS make time for . . .
and to Kyle who makes every day with them bearable! (Haha, kidding.)

In loving memory of my late grandmother Carol ("Gagy") Levitan. Every time I called Gagy, she would ask, "So? Write anything lately?" Yes, Gagy. And I wish you were here to read it. I know you're still watching over me.

TABLE OF CONTENTS

SEE FRIENDS

WRITE

LOSE WEIGHT

INTRODUCTION

I was sitting on the couch next to my thirteen-year-old daughter who was hunched over her phone. Every so often she would exhibit a series of spastic gestures, which I'd learned to rule out as a seizure and instead attribute to the latest TikTok trend. I didn't even think she was listening to us. My husband, Kyle, his dad, and his dad's fiancée were also scattered around the living room swapping ideas for this anthology's title.

Moms Don't Have Time To Two?! No, too derivative and it isn't a sequel.

Moms Don't Have Time To Sleep, Get Sick, Have Friends, Write, and Lose Weight? Too long.

We kept joking around, dismissing terrible suggestions, until my daughter, without even looking up from her phone, said, "Moms don't even have time to be moms."

I don't know if it was sleep deprivation or the late hour talking, but I thought it was the most profound thought ever.

"Ha!" I said.

"So true," said my father-in-law's fiancée.

"Hilarious," said Kyle.

We all agreed.

"It's so ironic," I said. "Without kids, we wouldn't even be moms."

"Well, there's your title," said Kyle. "Nice job!!" he said to my daughter.

And then, she finally looked up.

"What?"

The essays in this book are inspired by five things that moms don't have time to do. But this collection is not just for moms—it's for all of us. It's for everyone who is busy and struggling to prioritize the zillion competing demands on their time.

Unfortunately, getting sick is one thing I did find time to do. Several days before my last anthology book launch, I caught COVID-19. I spent nine days alone in bed with almost every symptom: loss of taste and smell, vertigo, cognitive fog, fever, cough, aches, dizziness, and fatigue. Not that I let any of this stop me from eating, mind you. A friend sent me a giant box of my favorite cookies. I took one bite, looked at it, and thought, "Ugh, this cookie has no taste!"

Oh, wait.

I debated internally. Should I still eat it!? I can't taste it or smell it but I know I should be loving it! I decided that I wouldn't deprive those pleasure sensors in my brain. So the section in this book on losing weight is, well, top of mind. (Top of thigh?)

Likewise, I don't think I've gone two consecutive, uninterrupted nights of sleep since my twins were born fourteen years ago, followed by their little brother and sister, eight and six and a half years later.

Seeing friends? Sounds great, rarely happens. I think I've spent more time emailing and planning to see friends than actually seeing them.

Most days, my Instagram posts are all I can find time to write. (Follow me: @zibbyowens.)

And yet, if we don't make time for the important things in life like sleeping, socializing, combating illness, staying fit, and writing, what's left? Without our friends, food, acknowledging our innermost thoughts, staying healthy, and getting a good night's sleep, we wouldn't even survive.

We must make time.

But how?

The following essays by dozens of bestselling and notable authors who have been on my podcast, *Moms Don't Have Time to Read Books,* are a literary ode to the things that are most important.

Life is short. We know that. So let's make time to enjoy it.

At the very least, let's make time to read these very short essays about the things that matter most. If not now, when?!

—Zibby Owens

MOMS
DON'T HAVE
TIME TO
SLEEP

The Year of Magical Sleeping

LYNDA COHEN LOIGMAN

I used to be home by myself a lot. My husband took an early morning train to the city and didn't walk back into the house before eight. My son was a busy high school senior and my daughter, a college junior, lived three hours away. During the early months of COVID-19, all of that changed.

My husband's office shut down, high school became remote, and my daughter's college told all of the students to leave. Soon, the four of us were together at home. The addition of my daughter's roommate made us a robust household of five.

Suddenly, I was no longer alone.

When my house became full, I could no longer sleep inside it. There were too many people on too many different schedules. There were too many noises, too much tumult. There were too many surfaces to disinfect and too many meals to plan. My brain was overheating. I was too anxious to relax. The idea of sleeping seemed absurd.

At night, I lay awake worrying about one of us getting sick. I lay awake worrying about my father in Florida, who seemed to think he didn't have to be all that careful. I lay awake worrying about my husband's father, a poster child for the term "underlying conditions." I lay awake worrying about all the milestone moments both my son and daughter were missing.

I lay awake, in part, because my husband was snoring.

My husband's snoring was nothing new. Depending on his weight, his stress level, and even what he'd just eaten, the intensity of it waxed and waned over the years. Normally, if the noise woke me during the night, I would grab my pillow and head for the extra bedroom over our garage. When the kids were little, before we had an extra room, one of us often escaped to the couch. But by mid-March, there were no more empty beds in the house. The couch was occupied by wide-awake young adults who stayed up too late and had worries of their own. Stress had brought my husband's snoring to a new decibel level and there was nowhere to go, no quiet place to be found.

On a visit to Washington, DC a few years ago, I shared a hotel room with my husband and my son. My husband's snores woke our son during the night, and in the morning we found him wrapped in his comforter on the floor of the bathroom, fast asleep. I called housekeeping to ask for a cot, and we set it up the next night inside the bathroom. On the day that we left, we had a good laugh thinking about what the hotel staff must have thought of us.

About a month into quarantine, as I listened to my husband's snores, I remembered that hotel and the cot in the bathroom. Whether it was the lateness of the hour or my own exhaustion, suddenly the idea didn't seem strange at all. I got up and went looking for our air mattress and found it, eventually, in the back of my closet. In a fit of sleep-deprived inspiration, I looked around the space and contemplated my options.

My closet was not particularly neat. The hangers didn't match. The sweater piles were sloppy. But it was surprisingly and wastefully wide. Maybe even wide enough to fit the air mattress. When I began to inflate it, the noise woke my husband who shuffled out of bed to investigate. He laughed when he figured out what I was doing. A grown woman could not sleep inside a closet, he said. I told him I disagreed.

I made up the mattress with twin sheets and a comforter. I brought in an extra pillow, my phone charger, and a book. That night,

I felt like Harry Potter in his cupboard under the stairs, but without a trace of Harry's loneliness or resentment. I fell back asleep, completely content. When I woke again, it was after eight in the morning. It was the first time I'd been able to sleep for weeks, and at the time, it felt like magic.

Throughout the spring and the summer, my closet became my favorite "room" in the house. Sure, I had to turn my "bed" onto its side to open my sock and underwear drawers, but that slight inconvenience was a small price to pay for such a peaceful space of my own. I rested better at night beside my husband knowing my closet was there if I needed it. When I retreated inside it (several nights a week), I slept until morning, undisturbed.

What started out as a place to escape all the noise took on an almost mystical appeal. My closet was the treehouse I had always wanted. It was the cozy pillow fort and the secret clubhouse I had dreamt about when I was a child. The strangeness and smallness of the space only made me love it more.

In winter, after months of lockdown, my full house became empty again. My daughter and her roommate returned to college. My son took a job and moved away from home. I put away the puzzles that had taken over the dining room, organized the pantry, and cleaned the refrigerator. The quiet took over, perhaps a little too fiercely, and I missed the raucous dinners and Netflix-filled evenings.

Now when my husband snores beside me, I have plenty of extra beds to choose from. The problem is I don't sleep well in any of them. The comfort I seek cannot be found in a soft swath of carpet or a fluffy duvet. It comes from knowing I have my own private sanctuary, no matter how small, surprising, or odd.

The past year has been a study in flexibility and a reminder of the importance of imaginative thought. If we are forced to do doctor's visits and Thanksgiving over Zoom, if our children must learn and grow in painful isolation, if we must manage uncertainty and process our collective grief each day, we can certainly do our best to create tiny magical spaces that offer us some of the peace and rest we all need.

It may not surprise you to know that I haven't put my air mattress away just yet. If you're ever looking for me after midnight, try knocking on my closet door.

Lynda Cohen Loigman is the author of the novel *The Two-Family House,* which was a *USA Today* bestseller and a nominee for the Goodreads 2016 Choice Awards in Historical Fiction. Her second novel, *The Wartime Sisters,* was selected as a Woman's World Book Club pick and a Best Book of 2019 by *Real Simple.* She is currently at work on her third novel.

Night Breathing

CARLA NAUMBURG

"I think you have a sleep disorder."

My husband said that to me on more than one occasion in the months after our second daughter was born. I ignored him, except, of course, when I accused him of mansplaining.

As much as I didn't want to admit it—to my husband, or myself—I suspected he might be right. I was tired all the time. No matter how many hours I slept, I inevitably woke up groggy, desperate for coffee. I dragged my way through each day, struggling to complete my tasks and stay patient with my kids. I bailed on evening plans with friends because I was completely depleted.

I tried to convince myself that debilitating fatigue was just part of the deal when you're a working parent with an infant and a toddler, but I knew it wasn't the truth. Our daughters each slept through the night by the time they were a few weeks old. I couldn't blame my exhaustion on them, as much as I may have wanted to.

So I continued to ignore my husband's ongoing suggestions that I talk to my doctor—I just couldn't deal. I was barely managing the basics of daily life; I had zero bandwidth available for anything else. I couldn't begin to imagine how I might tackle my sleep, much less the debilitating postpartum anxiety that kept me up at night or the pounds that piled on as I tried to boost my energy each afternoon with a chocolate-chip pumpkin muffin on the way to pick up my girls from preschool. What I didn't realize at the time was that my anxiety, my weight gain, and my sleep disorder were all pieces of the same fucked-up puzzle.

I don't remember what finally propelled me to make an appointment with a sleep doctor months later (the details of those early parenting years remain a blur), but I finally did. The doctor asked me a few questions about my sleep habits, weighed me (ugh), and measured my neck (an experience which I found just as humiliating as stepping on the scale). She sent me on my way with a home sleep study in the form of a small black case filled with straps and sensors. That night, after the girls were in bed, I strapped a thick stretchy heart rate band around my chest, forcing my significantly less-than-perky breasts even farther south. I wrapped yet another band around my forehead and clipped a heart rate monitor on my finger. My husband, of course, thought the whole thing was hilarious. If I weren't so damn tired, I probably would have agreed with him.

Despite having been poked and prodded through two rounds of IVF and giving birth to two nine-pound babies, I couldn't remember feeling less sexy, less feminine, and less proud of my body than I did that night—until, of course, I had to go through it all again a few weeks later.

The results from the at-home study were inconclusive, which was how I ended up in a hotel room. OK, it may have been a former hotel room that had been turned into a sleep lab and rigged up with sensors, wires, cables, and cameras. Whatever. I had two children under the age of three, so it could have been lined with compost and crocodiles for all I cared—it was a night alone and I was thrilled.

That was, until, the lab tech arrived. Don't get me wrong, she was friendly and efficient, but having over thirty adhesive sensors attached to one's head, face, and legs is gonna put a damper on any solo hotel-room experience. As much as I had hoped to relax and enjoy my night off from parenting, the pull of the adhesive in my hair, the sensors glued to my jaw, and the knowledge that a complete stranger was monitoring my every move from the room next door made it all a bit tricky.

I woke up the next morning feeling completely depleted. I needed a night off to recover from my night off, but sadly, that was unlikely to happen any time soon.

A couple of weeks later, I got a call from the doctor. I had a mild case of sleep apnea, a common sleep disorder that is often (but not always) the result of excess weight on the body. The doctor recommended I start sleeping with a CPAP (continuous positive airway pressure) machine, which was about the size of a shoebox that would sit on the floor next to my bed. A flexible hose attached to a piece of rubber I strapped around my head and placed under my nose, with two nipples that pushed a stream of air up each nostril in order to keep my airway open. The thing made me sound, and feel, like an overweight, middle-aged version of Darth Vader.

But dammit if the thing didn't work. I didn't realize how effective the CPAP was until about a week after I started using it, when I found myself running errands after the girls were in bed. I went to the FREAKING MALL. I don't even like the mall, but I was so excited to have enough energy to go that I went anyway.

I was ecstatic.

To be clear, I was ecstatic about my newfound energy. I continued to despise the CPAP, which felt like a nightly reminder of my failure to lose the baby weight and generally stay on top of my shit. My husband saw it differently. He loved that damn thing. Not only was I less cranky and reactive during the day, but I was a much quieter sleeper, which meant he got a better night of sleep, too.

It's now been almost ten years since I made that first trip to the sleep specialist. In the months and years that followed, I used my newfound energy to start exercising regularly. I started treatment for my anxiety, including therapy and antidepressant medication. I was able to lose much of the weight I had gained. And even though my CPAP machine is now gathering dust in the back of my closet, my sleep continues to be a major priority in my life.

Now, this is the part of the essay where I should be telling you how I learned my lesson, and now I'm religiously and consistently devoted to my self-care and always put my own needs first. Not quite. I'm still a working mother of two (now) tween daughters, and I still live in a society that gives mere lip service to women and mothers prioritizing their self-care. But I have come to believe that sleep is not only sacred, but it's also the foundation of my ability to function well in every single area of my life. And I'm grateful to be sleeping through the night more often than not—even if I'm still occasionally ignoring my husband.

Carla Naumburg, PhD, is a clinical social worker and the author of *How to Stop Losing Your Sh*t with Your Kids.*

Room for One

ALLISON PATAKI

I could read the surprise on my husband's face. He'd asked me what I wanted for my upcoming birthday and I'd answered quickly and simply: a night away. A night away from him, away from home, away from our daughters, our dog, our laundry—all of it. One glorious night in a hotel room by myself.

"Would you want to ask your mom to cover for us?" he asked. "So you don't have to go alone?" I responded with a decisive "No." He was offering to join me, but I didn't want him to. I didn't want *anyone* to join. I needed quiet. I needed rest. I needed just a few hours to tune everyone else out and tune in to myself. To exhale, to heal, to simply be, and most of all, to sleep.

The past three years had been tough—and exhausting. Shortly before the birth of our first daughter, my young, healthy, athletic husband, Dave, had suffered a massive stroke that had nearly taken his life. He'd survived, miraculously, but the year following that improbable health crisis and Dave's painstaking recovery had been one in which I'd cared tirelessly for both my husband and my newborn. Then, two years later, I rushed back to the ICU with another nonresponsive loved one, this time our second baby girl, just seven weeks after we'd welcomed her arrival. She, too, miraculously pulled through her own crisis. She came home with us and she was mercifully healthy. But at the end of it all, *I* was in pain. I felt bruised and worn. Motherhood, even in the best of times, is an exhausting job; my introductory years in the role had been harrowing.

Thankfully, Dave accepted my request with grace. Which is how I found myself, a few weeks later, driving ten minutes to an inn the next town over. I picked a place close enough that I could get home quickly if, God forbid, I needed to hurry back. But it was far enough—just getting out of the driveway allowed me to exhale. As I approached the front desk to check myself in, relief came gushing out. "It's my birthday!" I proclaimed. "I'm here by myself. I'm so excited! I'm a mom, and this is my first night to myself in over three years. I'm going to sleep!" The man behind the counter smiled wanly.

When the manager heard it was my birthday and saw how deranged with joy I appeared to be, he upgraded me. To a suite! I couldn't believe it. When I got to my room, there was a bathtub and a bottle of Champagne awaiting me. I shut the door, looked around to confirm that I was in fact alone, and I smiled. It was silent, and it was still. I'd made it.

I had nothing that I needed to do. No one who needed my care and attention. For the next eighteen or so hours, I could just be.

I took a walk around the hotel's lake, where the last of autumn's colors brightened a peaceful mountain landscape. I breathed deep the clean air and then I came back to the room and unfurled my yoga mat. As it got dark outside, I ordered beef tenderloin and some sort of cheesy potato deliciousness from room service.

I looked at the clock; at home, this was one of the most chaotic hours of the day. But there, in the hotel room, it was quiet and peaceful. It felt so luxurious to eat all of my dinner without interruption, to pass an entire meal without negotiating with small but mighty human beings about vegetable or ice cream intake. Afterward, I slipped into the plush hotel bathrobe and drew myself a bath. Ah, bath time. Not for my baby! Not kneeling on the mat singing "Baby Beluga," dodging errant splashes, the toweling and tooth-brushing and diapering. Just me, soaking in a warm tub, relishing total quiet and the unburdened, unstructured passage of time.

I got into bed. I stretched my legs across the empty space. It was the first time in many years that I'd had a bed to myself. I was alone, but I didn't feel lonely. It was just what I needed.

That night in that hotel room by myself, I said a prayer of gratitude. We'd been through a lot as a family. I'd been through a lot. It felt right to take this moment to rest and heal for myself. Alone in bed, I burrowed under the covers and I prepared for a long night of uninterrupted sleep. As I closed my eyes, I told myself that there was absolutely no reason that I needed to get up. I gave myself permission to rest—and to rest until my body awoke on its own.

I slept until just before nine o'clock the next morning, which was the latest I'd slept in years. After a quiet solo breakfast and another walk outside, it was time to return home. Pulling back into my driveway, I felt like the muscles in my body—including the most vital one of all, my heart—had unclenched. I had been gone less than a day, and yet those hours had provided me with the rest and quiet that I'd so desperately needed.

It's been three years since my first hotel night away, and the escape has turned into an annual birthday tradition. As I've healed and grown through these early years of motherhood, I've come to recognize that rest is a priority. Not only for my own physical, spiritual, and mental well-being, but for the health of my entire family.

As I sit here thinking about all of this, I remember that my birthday is a few weeks away. Time to call up a local hotel and book myself a night away, party of one. I won't go far, but simply the fact that I'm going shows me how far I've come.

Allison Pataki is the *New York Times* bestselling author of six novels, two children's books, and the memoir *Beauty in the Broken Places*. Allison's novels have been translated into more than twenty languages. She has written for the *New York Times*, *ABC News*, the *Huffington Post*, *USA Today*, and other outlets. A certified yoga instructor, she lives in New York with her husband, three children, and a rescue pup.

It's OK, I'm Awake

CECILY VON ZIEGESAR

Dear New Tenant in Apartment 2E,

While wind chimes make a lovely tinkling sound in a soft summer breeze, they can be quite LOUD in an early March Nor'easter with fifty mile-per-hour winds. One of the nicest things about our building, especially the apartments facing the back, is that it is QUIET. Your wind chimes disturb the quiet. I'm an extremely light sleeper. Would it be possible to tie up or take down the wind chimes at night?

Thank you for understanding.
—Your downstairs neighbor

I wrote that note over a year ago. Last month I bumped into the owner of the wind chimes. She smiled at my bedraggled face and said cheerfully, "You know, everyone always tells me how beautiful my wind chimes are. You don't still mind them, do you?" I stared back at her helplessly.

Did it matter, really, if she took them down, or not? I was awake anyway. I'm always awake. I lied in the note when I said I was a light sleeper. I'm not any kind of sleeper. The fact is: I don't sleep.

Here is a condensed list of things that keep me awake:

Ice cubes collecting in the freezer.

The dog's sighs.

The cat's sighs.
My husband's sighs.
The amount of computer gaming equipment in my son's room.
The college classes my daughter has to select for next semester.
The weird conversation I had with that oversharing guy I always see walking his dog about his marital problems and phantom illness—I don't even know his name!
The weird conversation I had with my mother.
The weird conversation I had with my stepmother.
The weird conversation I had with my mother-in-law.
The way the outlets in our house are all crooked.
My cell phone updating.
My computer updating.
My husband's and children's cell phones updating.
My husband's and children's computers updating.
The coat I wish I hadn't given away.
The search for the perfect jeans.
Are prairie boots still a thing?
The Staten Island ferry's horn.
Lightning over New Jersey.
My cell phone spying on me.
The bar on the corner rolling out kegs.
Stray cats' sighs.
Fear that if I fall asleep, I'll have that dream again where I'm a wolf in a wolf pack and I wake myself up, howling.
This shampoo smells weird.
This deodorant doesn't work.
This moisturizer makes me itchy.
The towels shed.
The dog sheds.

I need to file my nails.
Where will we be in ten years?
Are my children happy?
Why does the tap water smell like Clorox?
When was the last time I went to the dentist?
If the dog could talk, would he sound like Sean Connery or
  Daniel Craig?
I need to find a type of wine that doesn't keep me awake.
I should learn a new language.
Singing drunk people.
Singing birds.
Those damned wind chimes.

* * *

I could blame my sleeplessness on my children, on motherhood. The waking of hungry, distressed babies every few hours can disturb a mother's sleep patterns. But my children are big old teenagers. They sleep through the night, all morning, and well into the next day! Even when they were infants and would wake up and cry for milk or to have a diaper changed, I was awake anyway.

When my toddler daughter would sleepwalk out of her room and stand at my side of the bed in her nightie, staring straight ahead with big, unblinking, horror movie eyes, I would greet her, "Hello, my scary bunny. You're sleepwalking again. Let's go back to bed." And then I'd take her back to her room, and she wouldn't remember a thing. Neither would my husband, or the dog, because of course, they were asleep.

My son, when small, was a puker. Sometimes I made it to his room before the puke hit the bed and I could steer it to the floor. I did loads of laundry while everyone slept. It was invigorating. Again, my husband would be puzzled by the freshly laundered and folded sheets and pajamas in the basket outside my son's bedroom door. "Somebody shouldn't eat spaghetti with red sauce, ever," I would say. Or pizza. Or hot dogs. Or Halloween candy.

But those are the nights when there's something to do. Most of the time there's nothing but the quiet and me, and the ice, and the wind chimes.

I used to have a prescription for Ambien. I loved Ambien. I'd take it, my light switch would switch off, and I'd be out for four solid hours. But as soon as it wore off, I'd be wide awake, worrying about what happened during the time I'd missed. Was there a storm, a fire? Is the dog OK? My children? After my doctor advised me not to take Ambien every night, I stopped taking it altogether. It's addictive, you don't get the right kind of sleep, and it's possible to do crazy things while under its influence and not remember. The internet is full of wild Ambien tales. Luckily, we live in the city and our car is in an outdoor lot with a complicated gate a block away from our home. Otherwise, I might have driven to the airport, gotten on a plane, and married someone I met on the plane.

"Relaxed Mind" tea and two Benadryl put me to sleep for a couple of hours, but I'm groggy and cranky all the next day. Acupuncture might help if I went weekly, but the dog would feel neglected. I've never tried sleep therapy. I've never been to a sleep clinic. The thought of doctors watching me sleep keeps me awake.

As a writer who has not slept for fifty years, I have a private joke with myself when people ask how I think up my characters, my ideas. Writing for me is the closest thing to sleep. It's the only time I give up control and go into some kind of trance. This must be what sleeping feels like, what dreaming is. I wouldn't know.

OK, I do sleep sometimes—for an hour or two—otherwise I'd be dead. On my last birthday I passed out after dinner at the unfathomable hour of nine o'clock, after my kindly teenagers made me drink a takeout frozen margarita the size of a Big Gulp from the bar on the corner (where the singing drunk people hang out). At midnight the wind chimes, like a gong or an alarm, startled me awake.

The nap was refreshing. I got up to see what I'd missed.

Cecily von Ziegesar is the author of the bestselling Gossip Girl book series—the basis for the notorious hit TV show, as well as the novels *Cum Laude, Dark Horses,* and her latest, *Cobble Hill.* She lives in Brooklyn, New York, with her family.

On Napping

MICHAEL FRANK

The wooden heel of an open-toed sandal, black leather and well-worn, goes *smack* against the peg-and-groove flooring upstairs. We can hear the sound a room, two rooms—three—away.

My mother has thrown her shoe against the floor, hard. The sound means: Be quiet, boys. It means: Let me have this moment to myself.

She is napping. She naps nearly every day between three and four o'clock in the afternoon. Can we not be quiet for just those fifteen, twenty minutes? Can we not give her just that amount of time to herself, so that she can reset her day?

We are three boys: six, eight, ten. Then ten, twelve, fourteen. Older still. Sometimes we settle down just long enough for her to fall into a proper sleep; often, because we are *rambunctious,* we are *impossible,* we continue to play games, fight, crank up the music. "I'm still tired from giving birth to the three of you," she explains. Or: "Three boys in four years, it's amazing I ever get out of bed."

She offers these remarks jovially, but what can we understand about her need to take a pause in the middle of the day? We who have energy at a high pitch, from morning to night. We who are not in any way attuned to the different phases of the life of the body, to how long a day can sometimes feel, when you are on duty full-time, as she is. We think: *something must be wrong with her.*

Our mother is not the only napper we know. There's her brother, our uncle the screenwriter. After his morning stint at his Smith-Corona, followed by an unvarying lunch of raw cashews, sliced fruit, and graham crackers, he lies down on his bed with something called an eye patch, a dark blue satin oblong that mummifies the upper quadrant of his face. He claims that his eyelids do not close completely and never have.

Our grandmother is a napper too: She withdraws a crumpled Kleenex from her sleeve and tucks it behind her eyeglasses to block out the light; she can sleep anywhere, in any position. And our grandfather, long dead, but leaving a trail of stories and quirks behind him: When he napped, he unplugged the telephone and drew the curtains, got undressed and disappeared under the covers. Woe to anyone who made a peep at three o'clock in his house.

On the other side of the family, the opposite philosophy prevails: "There's plenty of time to sleep in the grave"—this is a dictum of my aunt, whose reservoirs of energy run so deep they might as well be fed by speed (and for a time in the sixties, were, in fact, I later learned: Dexedrine, 10 mg, prescribed by our family doctor, for when she needed a pick-me-up). "You don't want to be missing out on life, do you now, and in the *middle of the day* what's more?" Or my vigorous father, who goes from morning until night, walking (or jogging), working, playing tennis, cooking; the man never closed his eyes before dark until he turned eighty.

Growing up among these people, these two schools of thought, I believe that the path is obvious: I don't want to miss out on life. I want to be vigorous. I will never nap.

I nap all the time.

Five days out of seven, at least. Typically in my reading chair, after lunch, with an eye patch (not blue, not satin). Rarely in bed. With an alarm set for twenty minutes, thirty if following an insomniac night.

My brothers nap too: The middle one, who wakes up at two in the morning with an unquiet brain, reaches for his glasses, and opens his computer—he goes horizontal whenever there is a break in his workday. My younger brother lies down on the floor and sets his alarm for eleven strict minutes. This is his (expanded) take on the micro nap as prescribed by Salvador Dalí: Sleep upright with a key in one hand and place a metal plate at the foot of your chair; when you begin to sleep deeply your grasp relaxes, the key falls against the plate and makes a noise, and you wake up—presumably refreshed.

I started napping fifteen years ago, when I became a father. *You'll understand when you're a parent*—this was a frequent refrain of my mother's, and I used to disdain it, negate it. I can understand life perfectly well without having a child, thank you very much. But in this as in many (so many) matters, she was right: you start napping when you're a parent because, hello?—you're infinitely sleep-deprived, and because parenting is worrying, and because life requires from you new and abounding resourcefulness and patience. The consequences of your choices, the behavior you model, the language you use. It's draining to be responsible for helping to form (or: trying not to ruin) another human being.

Naps remedy fatigue, sure. That's the obvious thing to say about them. But many years into this—what to call it? Life protocol? Life habit?—I frame the conversation around the nap somewhat differently. I've come to understand the necessity of the restart, the do-over, or the second chance. The change in perspective that comes so readily to hand. A nap makes two days out of one. It has analogs in meditation, yoga, and exercise; it resets the body while allowing you to clear out mental tangles. As a writer, I go to battle with the tangles and the confusion most every day, and, being a glacially slow learner, I often stick with this battle when I would more productively turn sooner to the afternoon nap (or swim, or meditation). Because when I do nap, almost invariably I come back to my work, and my life, from a different angle.

It's so basic and so effective, and yet I keep forgetting the lesson. Even after all these years I continue to regard the nap as a discovery, just as I continue to think and speak about it with some shame.

Why in this culture of ours, the decidedly un-Mediterranean, *siesta*-less America, is there so much guilt about napping? The notion seems to go way back. Ben Franklin called nappers "sluggards"; he too invoked the grave. Thomas Edison regarded sleep generally as a bad habit and described naps as a "dip into oblivion"—even as he sometimes took two or three such dips every day. Yet JFK napped (in bed, with the curtains drawn tight and Jackie by his side), as did President Johnson, Albert Einstein, Winston Churchill, and Leonardo da Vinci.

Napping and the grave are one pairing you come across all the time; napping and depression is another. This depressive retreat into bed, to treat a deep unslakable exhaustion that possibly shouldn't even be described as exhaustion, strikes me as a very different kind of withdrawal than the afternoon pause; its goal is to detach from the world instead of preparing to rejoin it. The afternoon nap as I practice it is future-minded: You're napping because you have a plan for what you want to do when you wake up. It's about rebirth, reframing, recharging, revisiting, remaking.

With the arrival of COVID-19, I found the need for such regular restarts to be more acute than ever. The stream of anxiety and decisions we are faced with daily, everything from whether we should walk into Trader Joe's for a quart of milk or agree to send a child to an in-person school day, can feel so daunting and consequential. The nap is just the punctuation mark we need in this long sentence the virus has written into our lives; it's the semicolon that allows us to come at all these challenges from a new angle, to be careful and responsible without becoming paralyzed or giving up.

The subject of the nap comes, like the nap itself, with a coda: the point at which the nap ends, and you awake, a transition from unconsciousness to consciousness that has always seemed more mysterious to me, and more disorienting, than its start-of-day equivalent. To wake from a nap is to find yourself in an altered mental state so profound that it can feel almost drug- or sickness-induced. This interstice is a rich hunting ground for ideas, insights, and understanding—but you have to pay close attention. It comes on strong and fizzles out fast.

I'm not alone in my appreciation of the moment that closes out the nap. Consider this from Philip Roth: "The best part of it is that when you wake up, for the first 15 seconds, you have no idea where you are. You're just alive."

Alive—yes—and ready for whatever is coming at you next.

🕒

Michael Frank is the author of *The Mighty Franks,* a memoir, and *What Is Missing,* a novel, which was optioned by Morning Moon Productions. He is a 2020 Guggenheim Fellow.

When Bedtime Won't Come Soon Enough

ZIBBY OWENS

Time and I are like kids playing tag in the backyard. Usually time is chasing me and I'm racing through the freshly cut grass in my overalls, my heart pounding, my chubby legs pumping, narrowly escaping being grabbed by the bigger bully of a boy behind me. But occasionally we switch roles. Sometimes I'm the one who has to pursue time, left in the dust of a much more nimble opponent who knows the landscape, who expertly dodges trees and divots and discarded toys littering the lawn, leaving me out of breath and nowhere close to victory.

Saturday was one of those days. It was a day when instead of racing against the clock like I do during the workweek as podcaster/author/entrepreneur, trying to finish emails, calls, podcasts, meetings, anthology launch events, and books, I found the second hand had simply stalled.

Every time I looked at my watch, hardly any more time had gone by. I wanted to nudge it along so I could finally just get the kids to bed and go to sleep myself, but this round of tag was one I didn't stand a chance to win. The bully had beaten me. By a mile.

A few years ago, I had a last-minute hysterectomy due to a giant, rapidly growing fibroid in my uterus that doctors believed could potentially be cancerous. (Yeah, that was fun.) They went in and took out both the fibroid and the uterus, rearranging all my organs in the process, but left my ovaries, meaning I still have monthly hormonal cycles but no evidence that the hormones are the root cause of my occasional oppressive bouts of depression and irritability.

But there's a certain tint to those days when hormones are at least partially to blame, like an Instagram filter that makes everything in the image too dark, one that I'd try out and think, *Oh, definitely not this one; everything looks terrible!* There's a hopelessness and a heaviness to it, a physical pressure like a boot on my chest, a wellspring of tears at the ready like paparazzi outside a restaurant waiting for a Kardashian to emerge. *Click, click, click.*

Saturday was one of those days, when time turned on its heels and the tears came flooding out and I barked at everyone I loved and I couldn't make the day end soon enough. Which sounds particularly terrible because I know how lucky I am. I knew I was so lucky to be spending the weekend with three of my four kids, while the fourth spent "alone time" with his dad, my ex. I was so lucky to be spending the weekend with my adorable (second) husband who cooked dinner for all of us. I was so lucky that my husband's dad and his new fiancée, an angelic woman just four years older than me, were also there, entertaining the kids. My in-laws, who came to help soon after their engagement. And I was so lucky to be with my black lab, Nya, inherited recently from my late mother-in-law who succumbed to COVID last August. Nya has appointed herself my seeing-eye dog and waits at my feet while I type, sits by my side while I eat, lays on my legs as I sleep, and jumps up whenever I so much as touch my purse. I was so lucky that I could afford the bags of groceries I stuffed at King Kullen at 7 a.m., a loot that necessitated a mid-check-out run to the car because there were too many coarse brown paper bags to fit in just one cart.

And yet.

Time didn't care how lucky I was.

Time didn't care that I knew I was blessed.

Time was giving me the finger as he ran away.

All day I dragged. The internal motor that typically propels me at warp speed sputtered and cut off, and all mechanics were off duty. Nothing could jumpstart it. Nothing could get me to run faster in the back yard, to try to catch up to time. The day wouldn't progress.

It didn't help that my kids and husband were in what seemed like our eight millionth quarantine. After a recent exposure to someone we had all seen, we were waiting out day nine of quarantine, knowing that after four negative COVID tests, everyone was going to be fine but still required to be at home. I was the only one who could leave, having recently had COVID myself and spending nine days sick in bed.

But what good was that, really, if no one could come with me, and there was a collective outcry if I even went to walk the dog?

It didn't help that this week marked a full year since we originally went into hiding from the pandemic and my nerves were frayed, like the jeans from 1972 that my dad insists on still wearing. It didn't help that my husband and I hadn't spent a second alone together in weeks and that fear was hung like the mezuzah on our front door. It didn't help that we had all simply had enough.

Saturday, which used to be something I looked forward to, showed up like an eager child pulling on the sleeve of my robe before I could make a cup of coffee, an unwelcome guest with no structure, not even the dreaded yet dependable rhythm of remote school to carry me through the day.

Just time.

And so, as I managed iPad Roblox-policing, unloaded the dishwasher, did laundry, mustered the creative juices for charades with my younger daughter, had a karate-chopping pillow fight with my little guy, negotiated skin care regimens with my older daughter, drove to see my older son for just fifteen minutes, put away groceries, forced showers, made smoothies, and more, I did so feeling like I was balancing on one leg with a sandbag hanging from my neck.

Nothing, exactly, was wrong, as I unsuccessfully hid my tears while reading *Little Miss Mischief* to the kids at bedtime. Nothing, exactly, was wrong, as I listened to Anna Quindlen's *Nanaville* while driving to see my son. Nothing, exactly, was wrong as I underlined Melissa Bernstein's *Lifelines* while waiting for the little guys to drift off, prepping for a podcast.

And yet, everything was wrong.

So when I snapped a selfie at bedtime and posted on Instagram how exhausted I was, when the bully boy had run out of steam and I'd finally grabbed the back of his shirt and exclaimed, "Gotcha!" all I could do was add #saturdaysarenojoke.

Sadly and predictably, many other parents and grandparents scrolling and seeing my post in their own moments of exhaustion understood, commenting in a chorus of what should have been commiseration and cocktails among like-minded moms, but was instead a series of emojis and one line concurrences.

Because we all get it.

And we are all right there. A year into the pandemic. Lucky, but not.

Worn out.

Chasing time.

You're it.

🕒

Zibby Owens is the creator and host of the award-winning podcast *Moms Don't Have Time to Read Books.* She is a regular contributor to *Good Morning America* online and the *Washington Post*, and her work has appeared in *Real Simple, Parents, Marie Claire, Redbook,* and many other publications. She lives in New York with her husband, Kyle, and her four children.

MOMS
DON'T HAVE
TIME TO
GET SICK

While I Was Sleeping

CAMILLE PAGÁN

"Ma'am? Ma'am, did you hear me?"

I had, but my mind was spinning as I tried to process what she'd just said. Because it was the four words that I, like so many others, had spent most of 2020 dreading hearing:

"You have COVID-19."

"Sorry," I muttered. "It's just that . . . that makes no sense." And it didn't. It was October 2020 and my husband, two kids, and I had spent months taking every precaution—avoiding other family members and friends, religiously wearing our masks and hand-sanitizing to the point that our skin cracked. I'd only gotten a COVID test as part of routine pre-screening for an endoscopy; after a lifetime of no GI issues, I'd developed sudden and severe heartburn in August, and my doctor wanted to rule out any serious causes. (Spoiler alert: it was just stress.)

"Are you having any trouble breathing?" the nurse asked me.

I shook my head. I have asthma, so I was always paying attention to how my lungs felt, and they were fine. Moreover, I hadn't lost my sense of taste or smell. Admittedly, I did feel kind of run-down—not unlike coming down with a cold that hadn't quite hit yet. I'd assumed that feeling lousy was linked to anxiety, or maybe even heartburn.

"What now?" I asked the nurse.

"Now you go home and quarantine for ten days," she said.

I pulled my head back. In fact, I'm positive I gave her the kind of look I generally reserve for people who peddle tin-foil-hat-level theories. I knew that what she was saying was 100 percent accurate—but it still sounded nuts. "Away from my *family*?" I said.

"Unless they test positive, too, then yes," she said, before handing me a few pamphlets and sending me on my way.

As I drove home, I kept thinking to myself: *I don't have time to be sick. And there's no way my family can function without me.*

Except the nurse was right: They would have to. As soon as I explained the situation to them (with my mask on, of course), I shut myself in our basement with only my worries to keep me company.

My husband JP is a hands-on parent; I knew he was capable of caring for our children, who were nine and twelve. But . . . we were in the middle of packing for a move that was supposed to happen three weeks later. On top of boxing up our belongings, there were utilities to switch and financial forms to complete and donations to be made. And homework to help with and rooms to clean and meals to make.

I had so. Much. To. Do.

How would it all get done without me?

My husband and kids tested negative for the virus, which alleviated some of my anxiety. Those ten days were among the hardest I've lived through, however. As I waited to see if my fatigue morphed into anything worse, I listened to the pitter-patter of my family's footsteps over my head as they got on without me.

"What's the news of the outside world? Tell me everything," I'd joke to my husband when he met me at the top of the stairs to hand me a meal or a card our kids had made for me. He'd assure me that while he wasn't going out—the three of them were quarantined, too—he was making progress on packing and paperwork. It was impossible not to notice how exhausted he looked, but he kept reminding me that this would be over soon. Would it, though? The end seemed so far.

* * *

In the meantime, I tried to do it all from afar. I FaceTimed with my children to remind them to shower. I texted my daughter to see if she needed help with her homework. I checked in with our realtor and reminded my husband that I, too, was perfectly capable of ordering groceries online.

Then, about two days into my quarantine, something curious happened. I gave up on trying to orchestrate my family's life and let myself do the one thing I really, really wanted to do: sleep. I've always been a seven hour-a-night sleeper; suddenly I was clocking ten to eleven hours, with a nap or two during the day. My doctor told me it was further evidence that I had the virus (I'll admit—even though I had a PCR test, which is the gold standard, I was doubtful). She was probably right, and I have no doubt that sleeping around the clock helped my body recover.

But standing offstage in my family's life as the show went on without me had another benefit: It let me see just how capable my husband and children really were. Not only did JP handle schooling and digital doctor visits and countless other tasks; but my kids rose to the occasion, too. My daughter, who loves to cook, woke up a little earlier to make breakfast for everyone. My son made sure the dog was let out so she could run off her energy, and proudly informed me he was remembering to shower. They left little treats for me at the top of the stairs. Basically, they continually reminded me that yes, they missed me. But they were also just fine.

Ten days later, I emerged from the basement tired but otherwise healthy, and profoundly fortunate that my illness had been so mild. As for my family, they looked a bit worse for wear—yet as the four of us embraced each other, I could sense that we'd all grown over the past ten days.

But mostly, I'd been the one to grow. As mothers, we do so very much because we can. Because we think we should. Because who else will do it?

The rest of our families will. That's what I realized while watching my husband make lunch a few days after I finished quarantining. And as my children thanked him without being reminded to, a profound feeling of relief washed over me. There were piles of laundry waiting to be washed and sorted and put away. Bills that needed to be paid and forms that had to be filled out, and yes, an entire house that needed to be packed in preparation for our move. But for once, I wasn't stressed about all that work, because I finally understood that I wouldn't have to tackle it alone. By not doing, well, anything, I'd learned that I don't have to do everything.

◷

Camille Pagán is the #1 Amazon Charts and *Washington Post* bestselling author of seven novels and a journalist who has written for the *New York Times*, *Real Simple*, *Time*, and numerous other outlets. She lives in Ann Arbor, Michigan.

Bodies in Motion and at Rest

ANDREA J. BUCHANAN

The woman behind me is praying to Jesus to protect this flight.

Things I want to look up but can't because my phone is in airplane mode:

Pelvic inflammatory disease
Nausea post-antibiotics
Can antibiotics make you nauseous once you stop taking them?
How long can a UTI last?
Am I damaged forever?

The flight attendant goes through the motions of life-saving instructions, stalking the aisles with a seat belt held over her head, metal snapping into place, slack fabric becoming tight then falling away, a magic trick performed for no one.

The woman behind me is sniffling, heaving, wailing.

There are men on either side of me. One of the men was on the phone as we boarded, saying *I love you*. The other had tried to start a conversation with me, but I smiled absently and looked away. I'm wary, because they are men, and because I am always wary when surrounded by men.

My pelvis and back are filled with nausea. My stomach bloats. I look pregnant, but I'm on the eighth day of a never-ending period, so I know I can't be. Can you imagine: pregnancy, now? When all I want is for my body to stop subjecting me to its whims.

The woman behind me is given tissues and talked down by a friend who distracts her with celebrity gossip, with something amusing they watch on an iPad without headphones.

The *I love you* man reads the in-flight magazine, lingering on an article about an actress. "An attitude of gratitude helps me stay less stressed," shouts the call-out text. Does the actress remind him of his *I love you* person? The page turns and I see another bold red call-out, the actress's dazzling face, as though she's laughing at a joke. "It's always been about acceptance."

The other man tents his fingers around his temples. He hasn't tried to talk again. But that doesn't mean he's given up. I put my headphones on. A flimsy barrier.

"Jesus protect us," says the woman behind me.

We are in the air.

* * *

My body has become a finicky houseplant: too warm or too cold as it revolts. My lips swell. My face becomes flushed and blotchy. My insides bloat with nausea. My limbs become 100 percent made of pure, organic ache. To survive I must lead a temperate, climate-controlled existence, out of direct sunlight.

Sunlight is my nemesis. Even in the shade, merely existing in the midst of photons is enough to trigger me, transforming my lips into *Real Housewives*–levels of exaggeration, my face a red butterfly mask.

Also my nemesis: food, but not all food and not all the time.

Also my nemesis: medication, even antibiotics I've taken before without any problem.

Also my nemesis: elevated heart rate. Whether from exercise or stress or, yes, even sex.

My worst nemesis of all: being alive in my own body.

Because sometimes, even without provocation, my body decides it has had enough. My tongue swells and tingles, my throat narrows; my body decides to let my arms feel detached from it, to let my heart pound with impending doom, to let my brain flood with a vaguely panicky sense of myself as "off," or "wrong," or "dying."

Or it mimics a UTI, cruelly performing the sensation of urgency, of burning; of persistent, dull kidney ache; of fever; of what the doctors politely refer to as "pelvic discomfort," which in fact feels experientially like my ovaries trying to claw their way out of me through my abdomen.

Or it simulates a heart attack, complete with oppressive pain-pressure in the center of my chest, radiating around to my back, trailing down my arm.

But it's never actually a heart attack, never a true UTI, never a true allergy. The call, as it were, is coming from inside the house. It's just my body, reacting to itself. My body, acting.

* * *

Hours later, out of the darkness and silence of the nighttime flight comes an announcement: "If anyone on board is a doctor, nurse, or paramedic, please report to the rear of the plane. A passenger needs medical attention."

The lights come on and passengers crane their necks to see what could be happening.

The woman behind me stands; her panic attack long since subsided. She's a nurse, she announces. Should she go back there?

A flight attendant tells her no. There are sounds of commotion. The lights on the plane's wings flash in my window, a pulsing warning.

I think about the woman behind me, a secret nurse. About me, a passenger secretly in need of medical attention.

My bladder and pelvis and lower back roil with nausea. I'm afraid to return home and take another UTI test, afraid to watch the test strip bruise into a deep purple again as it has for so many months.

What is wrong with me?

* * *

You've had a UTI. You know the rules of it, how if you get a fever of over 101 degrees, you have to go to urgent care in case it has gotten to your kidneys and turned into pyelonephritis. You know the test strips to buy in CVS, know the dread of them darkening the minute you dip them into your urine. You know how much it burns, how the minute you stop peeing, you feel like you have to pee again. You know how the pain is so distracting you can't focus on anything else except the raw ache in your pelvis, your bladder, and the dull kick in your back.

Imagine that persisting through months of antibiotics. Through an ER doctor suggesting that maybe your pain is from a pulled muscle, even though the urine strip is right there, purple as the wine-dark sea. Through the pelvic exams where you were told that probably you'd had so many UTIs (though technically this is your second, ever) that you gave yourself pelvic inflammatory disease and needed vaginal Valium—yes, that's right, you heard me correctly, Valium that you shove up your vagina in order to calm down, because really the problem is you are a woman and you just need to relax.

Imagine it persisting even as you store the arsenal of bullet-like Valium pellets in the refrigerator and nightly place them in your body, as directed, until you have what's called a "paradoxical reaction" and become suicidally depressed.

Imagine on top of all that, the anaphylaxis, your body responding to normal events like eating, like ovulating, like being outside in the sun, like medicine, as though they were lethal threats. Imagine your heart aching in your chest like an argument, with the kind of painful symptoms that, when you type them into Google, result in an instant list of websites indicating that you're going to die.

I'd hoped I was recovering on this trip, but I feel the dull ache in my gut as my body begs to differ. Perhaps I should stop fighting this. Perhaps, like the actress in the in-flight magazine article, I should cultivate an attitude of gratitude. It's always been about acceptance.

* * *

The man on my right makes conversation with the woman across the aisle. The man on my left writes an email. The nurse behind me is quiet, and the captain announces our descent. We all flex our jaws, popping our ears to ease the pressure, put away our electronic devices, and assemble our bodies to move off the plane as quickly as possible.

"Thank you, Jesus," the nurse behind me says as we land. She clutches her chest. I clutch my belly. We all hold our bodies together as we take our leave from each other, as our phones chirp and buzz and chime with the messages we missed while we were gone. A man crowds the aisle and frowns at a woman in his row. "I've traveled enough to know how to get off a plane," he snaps, his eyes drifting away from her before he even finishes his sentence.

The airport is midnight empty as I walk toward ground transportation. A cab takes me home but becomes ensnared in traffic. Soon we see the cause: a motorcycle on the ground. Six cars in disarray, one flipped. We crane our necks like plane passengers trying to see what's wrong. Young men standing, bodies in poses of grief. Hands on their foreheads, on their baseball caps, over their mouths in the middle of the freeway, police lights flashing their skin blue, then red.

My stomach tightens as I realize I have been spared yet another disaster. And then I am home, cats circling my legs. I pee on the UTI strip and watch it darken, a police light flashing purple. I knew it; I knew my nausea and pain weren't nothing. I knew it was real.

I close my eyes and for a moment it feels as though I'm still on the plane, soaring through the darkness.

Andrea J. Buchanan is the *New York Times* bestselling author of eleven books, including *The Beginning of Everything* and *The Daring Book for Girls.* Before becoming a writer, Andrea was a concert pianist. She currently lives in Philadelphia with her family.

In Spanish, I Don't Have Cancer

KJ DELL'ANTONIA

How do you say "cancer" in Spanish?

Any language student could make an educated guess at the answer to that question. Cancer, the illness, has been with the world for most of recorded history. Cancer, the word, dates back to at least Hippocrates. Much of our scientific language is rooted in that past. It's easy enough to do the math.

If you want to.

Not long ago, but back in the days when one could do this sort of thing, our family travel life suddenly began to revolve around Spain. Close friends moved there temporarily. We hosted a Spanish exchange student. My oldest was planning a gap year there. But when we visited, I became mute, my semi-decent command of French a hindrance rather than a help. I had to cede all control of our travels to my Spanish-speaking child or to the nearest Anglophone, and I didn't like it. There was only one thing to do: learn to speak Spanish.

My diagnosis with breast cancer coincided so closely with that decision that, looking back, I can't remember which came first. I went to have a lump checked. I downloaded a language app. My doctor decided that I needed a mammogram. I looked up online classes. The technician, contrary to all stereotypes, failed utterly to keep an impassive face and instead went to get her boss, who said that while someone would call me later to confirm, "There really isn't anything else that could be."

Maybe, at that point, the obvious next move should have been to cancel everything and devote myself to the full schedule of tests and consults and second opinions that appeared on my calendar, but that's not what I did. Instead, I found the biggest gap I could and made plans to join family friends in a return to Madrid.

My husband threw himself into learning the language of my illness. I threw myself into learning the language of vacation. Lobular, stage 2, invasive. *Soy, eres, es, somos, sois, son*: I am, you are, we are, they are. Lumpectomy, mastectomy, hormone receptors, protein receptors, radiation, tamoxifen. *Comer*, to eat. *Viajar*, to travel. *Trabajar*, to work. *Vivir*, to live.

I drove myself through the snow to my appointments while responding to the narrator in my new Pimsleur language app. *You are a woman visiting Mexico. Tell your hosts where you are from.*

Soy de América.

Now ask your hosts if they are from here.

Usted es de . . . aquí?

It takes a great deal of concentration to do this while driving. Far too much to think very hard about your destination. My husband met me at the hospital, and there it was his turn.

You are a man whose wife cannot formulate a coherent sentence. Now ask the doctor how panicked you should be. Take notes.

Our trip to Spain came in late spring, after my MRI and more biopsies and before I'd made as much progress with the language as I'd hoped. I could communicate basic ideas. I could tell people who I was, where I was from, and how many children I had. I could ask for directions, although I could rarely understand the answers. I could order in a restaurant if the server didn't stray too far from the Pimsleur-approved script.

It was wonderful. Everything we had left at home faded away in the pressure to conjugate verbs and put the right gender to nouns, and I spoke Spanish with anyone who would put up with me. We met the family of our exchange student. We had drinks with friends of our friends. I conversed gaily and resolutely in the only way I could: present tense, simple sentences. As far as my Spanish friends were concerned, that was all there was to me. No past, no future. Those ideas were too difficult to express. Only now.

At night, my husband held my hand in the European version of a king-size bed: two twins, held together by a sheet but with an uncomfortable gap between them. We waited for my phone to ring with the results of my latest tests and scans, which came in a metro station in Madrid: good news. The cancer was limited, and the oncology team had planned and scheduled my treatment. There really was only one thing to do at that point. I'd spent the flight to Spain immersed in my language studies. On the way back, I watched Netflix.

I went home to surgery and recovery and to months of hesitating over every English conversation in a very different way. *How are you?*, an acquaintance would ask after I was well enough to go out, and I would pause, stuck. No one wants an answer like mine in between the frozen food and the deli counter, but no one wants to find out later that you said fine when you most certainly were not. I missed Spain. No one there would ever question that I was *bien* in response to their *¿Que tal?*, because no one expected me to be able to say anything else.

Our oldest son left for a year in Spain in August, becoming the exchange student himself, living with our student's family. I went to radiation therapy five days a week and met three times a week with an online Spanish tutor, and in October, after my last session, we got on a plane and flew back to Madrid. On my first morning in the hotel, I turned over a newspaper that lay on a counter, wondering how much I would understand. One headline, at least, I could read easily: *Octobre era el mes de conciencia del cáncer de mamá.*

Part of me always knew that the Spanish word for cancer was *cáncer*, even if it came with a classy accent mark. There are over a thousand cognates between English and Spanish (words that are the same in both languages). I'd suspected all along that I could have made my situation understood. I just didn't want to.

We planned to go back to Spain this past summer. COVID-19 changed that, as it has changed so many things. Even so, my Spanish teacher recently declared me ready to tackle *el preterito*; now that I am able to discuss what I have eaten (*he comido*) and what I ate (*comi*) I'll soon progress to what I will eat in *el futuro*, after the pandemic, when I return to Spain.

Because this past fall, wearing my mask and wildly applying hand sanitizer at every turn, I went back for another mammogram. For luck, I listened to Pimsleur again.

Imagine you are on a beach vacation.

Yes, please.

You are ill. Tell the hotel clerk that you need a doctor.

¿Y tú, Pimsleur? Estoy infirma. Necesito un médico.

But for the moment, at least, I am not ill. This new scan found nothing. My *cáncer de mamá* has not returned, for now. I have a past, and a future, and I'm learning to talk about both.

⌚

KJ Dell'Antonia is the author of the instant *New York Times* bestseller *The Chicken Sisters*, a Reese Witherspoon book club pick, and of *How to Be a Happier Parent: Raising a Family, Having a Life, and Loving (Almost) Every Minute*. She is the former editor of the *New York Times' Motherlode* blog and the co-host of the *#AmWriting* podcast. She has to go outside every day, or else she—and her dogs—will go slightly insane.

A Small, Shiny Thing

KRISTY WOODSON HARVEY

On our way home from dinner at the local fish camp each week, my grandfather would often stop to buy me Luden's throat drops at a ramshackle gas station decorated with ancient metal signs proffering Coca-Cola and Pennzoil. The cherry treat was scarcely more than sugar and a little fruit pectin, but it made school days—where candy was strictly forbidden—much sweeter. Every week I'd wonder, excitedly, nervously: Was he going to stop?

Did he remember?

Perhaps that's why, in all those years as that little girl in her plaid jumper, I never lost my voice. And I would never have imagined my larger-than-life grandfather—in his pressed suit and wingtips—could have lost his.

That voice had talked to me over plates of biscuits and gravy at City View on Saturday mornings. It led bank board of directors' meetings that I witnessed from his lap and told stories of his "girlfriend," his great love: my grandmother.

He was a strong leader, an imposing man, an intimidating figure. But, to us, to his family, he was kindness and love wrapped in a package too big to ever fail.

His mind had been declining for a few years when they did the brain surgery that went badly, that took him away almost all at once. Illness, as it turns out, is a thief of many things—including memories. It can twist and turn them, distort and deface them. Or, in my case, it can remove them all together. My grandfather's illness had taken my remembrance of a man devoted and protective, strong and sure, and replaced them with this painful present.

Every now and then, he would come back in bright and blazing glimpses. When my grandmother broke her hip, he directed the firemen that came to her rescue. When I turned thirty, he called to wish me a happy birthday.

Doctors spent considerable time wondering what was going on inside his head. Was he gone or simply unable to communicate? And, more important, did he know who we—his family—were?

Did he remember?

I always believed he did.

At his funeral, people came from far and wide and stood outside the chapel in the halls, a testimony to the person he was. Friends who had known him for ninety-plus years told stories of his childhood. A former female employee reminisced that he promoted her to a position previously only held by men. A stranger said my grandfather had taken a chance on him and changed his life.

And then there were the dollars. Every day in his retirement, as he and my grandmother made their way around town, Grandaddy handed a gold dollar coin to every child he saw. Heavy and shiny, they were a kind of treasure that no piece of paper ever could be.

It was a gift, a surprise, and a lesson on how some things would be worth more in the future if they were saved. I heard from adults who had entire collections of gold dollars from years of encounters with my grandfather, children who had hoarded them for a special treat. Perhaps most notably, his minister referenced those dollars in a devotion, comparing this small act of selfless generosity to God's grace. Something neither expected nor earned or, quite often, even deserved. But something given out of love, all the same.

His grandchildren, Christmas after Christmas, day after day, were not only recipients of that unreasonably unconditional love. We were also recipients of that precious and weighty gold.

Last Christmas, the first Christmas without him, it seemed that without him there as he was, I could finally remember him as he had been. My memories returned in vivid Technicolor: sitting in Grandaddy's office window watching the Christmas parade with its music and dancing, tinsel and twinkle lights; fishing with cane poles, the surf roaring, the smell of the salt air; sharing a plate of Parker's barbecue and corn sticks, the spicy saltiness obscured by the deep knowledge that we were having our last real conversation. And rarely do I remember my grandfather as happy as when he sat beside the angel-topped Christmas tree, handing out presents to his children, grandchildren, and great-grandchildren.

That Christmas, there were presents. But there was no Grandaddy to hand them out. There were no gold dollars.

With the wrapping paper of at least twenty-five gifts for as many people strewn about the living room, an explosion of gold paper and red ribbon, shiny sparkles and patent bags, I retreated to my bedroom to put our treasures away, lest they be lost in the fray.

Inside my suitcase, what had begun as neatly stacked rows of pajamas and leggings, turtlenecks and toiletries, had become a chaotic mess. But when I lifted the top, the mess wasn't what I saw.

A small, shiny thing glinted. In the center of the pile, face up, deliberate, lay a brand-new gold dollar. Not fallen or slipped, left behind or forgotten.

Outside the bedroom door, the clatter of pots and pans in the kitchen, the running feet of children, and the laughing voices of those I loved blended into a cacophony. No, a symphony all my own—Christmas number thirty-four.

One voice—the biggest, most booming one, in fact—seemed to be missing. But, as I picked up the dollar, as I turned it over in my hand to make sure that it was real, that it was there, that I wasn't dreaming it, I realized that, though his voice may be missing—though it might have been missing for years—*he* was there. My grandfather was there.

I closed the dollar in my palm. He had left it.

He remembered.

So did I.

Kristy Woodson Harvey is the *USA Today* bestselling author of nine novels, including *Under the Southern Sky,* the Peachtree Bluff Series, and the forthcoming *The Wedding Veil.* She is also co-creator and co-host of the weekly web show and podcast *Friends & Fiction* and blogs with her mom, Beth Woodson, on *Design Chic.*

I Am Not Broken. Today, I'm OK

SHELLI R. JOHANNES

I've always been a healthy person. Besides suffering a broken heart at thirty, I rarely caught a cold and could count how many times I'd had the flu. On the rare occasion I got sick, I cured myself with chicken soup and an "I'm fine" attitude.

One day, everything changed.

On the cusp of my fortieth birthday, I woke up with ear pain. What started out as a little dizziness and discomfort became unbearable and debilitating, forcing me to consult a doctor. Over time, that minor ear infection caused extensive damage that left me battling vertigo for three years.

Some days, it felt like I was trying to balance on a rocking boat. (Did I mention I hate boats?) Other times, it felt like I'd consumed one drink too many. (And why I rarely drink today.) Driving was impossible and focusing on anything took all my energy. Instead of exercising or playing with my kids, I had to lie flat every chance I got to keep from throwing up. Over the next few months, I had doctor appointments, head scans, ear therapies, and head manipulations—none of them offering answers.

No cure. No remedies. No end in sight.

Doctors advised me to "wait and see."

It was the first time in my life I'd faced incurable health issues. The first time I lost faith in doctors and medicine. And, the first time I was petrified something was fatally wrong.

Over time, I lost myself to this chronic condition. I couldn't exercise and gained twenty pounds. I felt disconnected and isolated from family and friends. I struggled to work or write. I tried to convince myself that it could be worse, or that it would go away. After all, I'd always been healthy. Thin. Fit. And, aside from having two C-sections, even my pregnancies were "easy" (as if that's a thing!).

Desperate to heal, I turned to holistic methods like acupuncture, meditation, sound therapy, and energy healers. Then one day, my vertigo mysteriously vanished. Its absence left me consumed with anxiety and a deep-rooted fear that the illness would return. Afraid of setting it off, I quit yoga, never bent over, and never tilted my head. I slept on my back, rejected invitations, and hardly traveled.

I became a hypochondriac and let another chronic illness consume my life—fear.

Eventually, I went to therapy. Slowly, I came back—not just physically, but mentally. I lost the weight and reconnected with my family. I turned away from fear and lived life again—I even started going to yoga. For a couple of years, I was "me" again.

Then I turned forty-five.

One day in a carpool, a dull ache started to flare up in my left leg. I assumed I'd overstretched it in yoga. By the weekend, the pain traveled to all my limbs. Within days, I was writhing in pain—an intense level I'd never experienced, as if someone were scraping burning knives down every inch of my body. That night, I drove to the emergency room and was rushed back and put on a pain drip while doctors searched for answers.

As I lay there waiting for a diagnosis, I cried, petrified of what this illness could be. When my doctor returned with no answers, I remember thinking: *Not again*! The possibility of suffering through another chronic issue left me panicked.

For the next six months, the intense pain continued. I found myself back in doctors' offices. Brain scans. Spinal taps. Body MRIs. I was checked for autoimmune disorders and allergies. I had my nerves "tested," and was poked and prodded again and again, only to be handed another question mark.

The doctors guessed as much as I did: "Maybe it was anxiety," or "Maybe it was all in my head." But I knew my body. The continual, unabating pain was not a figment of my imagination. It was real.

I sought second and third opinions. I needed a name. A diagnosis. Something to look up. To Google. To learn about. To find my own cure. I needed a label.

I was frustrated and scared. I felt so alone.

Finally, I found a neurologist who listened and gave me a diagnosis: peripheral neuropathy and fibromyalgia. Basically, my nerves are damaged and don't send the right signals to my muscles—but no one knows why. I get fatigued easily and have extremely painful days where it feels like a truck has run over my body. Twice. I'm either tired or sore.

And sometimes, even a hug hurts.

My doctor prescribed medicine that helped manage the pain, but those dreaded twenty pounds came back (along with my Weight Watchers membership). I struggled to take medicine, always weighing pain levels against numbers on a scale (a balance I still grapple with today).

But besides the weight and frustration, this time was different. This time, I refused to let a chronic issue consume my life. This time, I fought the fear.

In 2020, I turned fifty.

I'm still in pain often (with bouts of vertigo), but I have come to terms with my health. I've realized that sometimes we don't get the answers we need. Sometimes, things don't make sense. And, sometimes, we have no control. It has taken me a long time to accept that this chronic condition is just a part of me, but it doesn't define me.

I have good days, but there are many bad ones where I feel broken. Anxiety makes it worse. But I know what I need to do to be OK: I need to be grateful, I need to have faith, and I need to take care of my body every day. Eat right, sleep eight hours, and walk. I need to laugh. I need to write. And no matter the weight, I need my medication.

I don't know what tomorrow will bring, but there are a few key mantras I try to live by and I repeat them to myself often: I'm not broken; I'm whole; I'm strong; and today, I'm OK.

Shelli R. Johannes is the author of teen novels and children's books including *Theo Thesaurus, Shine Like a Unicorn,* and is coauthor of the Loves Science picture book series. She can often be found on highways and country roads saving strays and jaywalking critters, or volunteering with animal conservation groups. Shelli lives in Atlanta with her husband, two kids, one bird, two crazy-haired golden doodles . . . and one huge imagination.

Walls in Our Minds

LILY KING

My daughter Calla reads to me aloud from her laptop screen:

> Illness is the night-side of life, a more onerous citizenship. Everyone who is born holds dual citizenship, in the kingdom of the well and in the kingdom of the sick. Although we all prefer to use only the good passport, sooner or later each of us is obliged, at least for a spell, to identify ourselves as citizens of that other place.

Her professor has sent her this passage after her review board this morning. It's from *Illness as Metaphor* by Susan Sontag. I can see that these words have given her power. There's an electricity coming off her. She has been wrestling with illness and art all semester, and here is a comrade in arms.

It's December 2020, and we are all, all over the world, in the thrall of COVID-19. Our lives have become narrow and enclosed, and my daughter is in a box within a box, her own private illness a smaller Russian doll nesting inside the public pandemic.

* * *

Like most college students, Calla came home last March. She'd been at an art school in London for six weeks—the beginning of a junior semester abroad—before the program shut down. They were the best six weeks of college she'd had so far. She'd come out of her shell in London; in a month and a half she made more friends than I could keep track of and she said yes to everything—a trip to Paris, a twenty-four hour drawing festival in Antwerp, a weekend in Florence. She and her friend Amy took surreptitious photos of Jude Law in a café in Primrose Hill. She drew Greek sculptures at the British Museum, saw several plays, and landed a job at an art gallery. She had one date with a very tall med student.

The day after that, her program was canceled, and two days later she flew home. I picked her up at Logan Airport in Boston, handed her a mask, and Purelled her hands. We headed north to Maine. Her eyes above the mask scanned the gray New England landscape on either side of the car and then looked at me full of shock. "What is happening?" she asked more than once.

Her sister, Eloise, had come home from New York a few days earlier, equally stunned. They both finished up their college semesters on their computers in their bedrooms. Instead of the summer restaurant jobs they were planning to get, Eloise started her own custom video company, and Calla got a job at a farm a few towns to the north. The farm job was five hours a day of physical labor: hauling irrigation pipes, unsheathing fields covered by enormous tarps, digging, planting, weeding, harvesting.

Within a few weeks her slender body was transformed. Her arm muscles bulged; her leg muscles became thick ropes beneath the skin. Her shoulders, once narrow and curled inward, broadened and realigned. From behind she was unrecognizable. She started listening to Buddhist and nonduality podcasts as she worked the land, which she told us made her think about existence, about human life, and the earth that sustains it. On the way home from work, she'd stop at a beach for a swim. She'd come through the door damp and pulsing with life. She'd lost London and new friends and travel adventures, but she found another kind of exploration, another way of thriving.

I look back on that first part of her summer with sadness. She had her health, a bursting physical and existential strength. But I can also see that these things were preparing her for the next setback.

On a Thursday in late July, she woke up with a headache and a fever. She didn't get better over the weekend, or the next week, or the next. COVID-19 tests were negative. Lyme disease was the most likely cause—every day, she'd peeled off ticks from her legs and arms at the farm. She'd tested negative for Lyme, too, but the doctor said that sometimes the antibodies don't show up for months.

Three weeks of the antibiotic doxycycline relieved Calla of her headache, but it didn't make her better. She moved from bed to couch to bed for most of August. Her new muscles shrank; her shoulders narrowed. I took Calla's temperature, made her favorite meals, and read to her at night. After she went to bed, I scoured the internet for answers.

We had come to the end of the road with traditional medicine. Calla entered the world of chronic, or treatment-resistant, Lyme, an upside-down world with its own test, co-infections, and vocabulary. A place where alternative-medicine practitioners go hard with the drugs, often prescribing two or three antibiotics at a time for months, if not years.

* * *

At the beginning of September, Eloise returned to New York, but Calla couldn't move into the apartment she'd found with a friend in Boston. Online classes started: her senior year. By then the fevers were gone, but she was still dizzy, weak, and exhausted at nine in the morning. She had muscle pain and a thick brain fog. She says now she doesn't remember the first week of Zooms.

Her new Lyme doctor told her that she was in the "early days" of the disease and that the road to recovery would be up and down; it would not be a straight line. In the letter he enclosed with the many supplements he sent her to go along with two antibiotics he prescribed, he drew a line that rose and fell across the page like a sound wave. Calla loved that he had made this simple drawing.

For the first part of the semester, she did not feel well most of the time. Most of her classes were in the morning; she napped in the afternoon. I worried that she was too sick to do the work. Then one day in October, I found her in her bathroom, filming for her animation class. There was a new brightness in her eyes, a quickness in her limbs as she moved. She'd made a short video montage of all her pill bottles, starting with the first antibiotic, then adding the herbals and the supplements. She'd started to let the sickness into her art. I could feel the power this gave her, the control. The illness was *useful* to her now, the art pushing things up and out of her.

The montage became part of a four-minute video called "Walls in My Mind." There is a voiceover and series of stills of drawings and paintings, collages and photographs. "There are walls in my mind," she says at the end, while stills of twelve small drawings of interiors, moving slightly from shot to shot, seem to be trembling together as if in a wind.

* * *

As her doctor had predicted, Calla's health rises and falls, though now, here in late December, the dips seem briefer, the swells longer. A few weeks ago, when she started to feel worse again after a month-long upswing, I said, "I'm so sorry. You must be discouraged." I tried hard to hide the disappointment on my face.

"No," she said, "it's how he said it would be." She made the up and down line with her hand in the air. "Also, it's still early days."

It's been five months, I did not say.

My own moods rise and fall with her health, but Calla's do not.

When she is not feeling well, I retreat even further from life outside the house. I'm slower to answer friends' texts, go on fewer masked walks. I spill out all my worries in my husband's arms at night and pray fervently for her in the morning. But she stays steady. She takes her pills and supplements twice a day, she does her work, makes her art, never complains. She takes walks with her mask on and earbuds in, listening to her nonduality podcasts. She says the philosophy has helped her undo a lot of attachment to superficial concepts like appearance, material things, and what people think of her. It's helped her to understand that she is not just a body, and this helps her to not identify as the body that is sick, so that she can be curious and interested in the sickness as a passing experience.

Early on, a friend of mine, whose daughter has had Lyme for seventeen years, wrote to me: "Illness is a teacher."

I'm not sure it is possible for me to not identify with this body that is a mother, a mother of two children, one who is unwell.

But Calla is learning from this illness, and I am learning from her.

◷

Lily King is the *New York Times* bestselling author of five novels, including most recently *Euphoria* and *Writers & Lovers*. Her work has won numerous prizes and awards, including the Kirkus Prize, the New England Book Award for Fiction, the Maine Fiction Award, a MacDowell Fellowship, and a Whiting Award, and she has been a finalist for the National Book Critics Circle Award and the PEN/Hemingway. She lives with her family in Maine.

Sick Leave

CAROLINE LEAVITT

I always knew exactly how we were going to raise our first baby, Max, and what kind of mother I would be. We knew we'd never shout or yell or belittle but would lavish love and encouragement. We'd read and talk to Max all the time. We'd show him the world. Every moment, we were sure, was going to be a miracle.

I had a blissful pregnancy, an easy delivery, and three perfect first days with Max. But right before I was due to go home, I suddenly became critically and mysteriously ill.

I was bleeding to death, and in such fierce pain the doctors put me into a medically induced coma for three and a half weeks as they tried to keep me alive. I had five emergency surgeries; my veins were glued shut, and then finally, a world-famous hematologist discovered my illness: a rare blood disorder that kept my blood from clotting.

When I was taken out of the coma, the first thing I saw on my hospital room wall was this huge blown-up photo of my son with a message: I miss you Mommy. Get well.

I was wired to machines, getting blood transfusions every hour and on morphine drips that made me hallucinate everything from Madonna to the nurses singing musicals. "I have to see my son!" I cried. I knew how important those first days of bonding were, but the doctors were adamant. "You're too ill," they said. Any movement could cause me to bleed out again, and they knew so little about my illness they were concerned I could give it to Max. "I have to see my baby!" I screamed, but they left, unmoved.

It was my husband, Jeff, who came to my rescue, coming in one day with a videotape of Max's first days: his first bath, his little body glossy as a pearl, his first trip to the doctor, his nap. The nurses gave up their break room so we could sit and watch, me in my wheelchair, an IV attached to my arm and Jeff beside me, holding my hand. I cried and cried, partly because of the wonder of the baby, and partly because Max was a stranger.

"I want to see him," I kept saying. "I have to."

But that didn't happen until four months later when I was released from the hospital, my numbers just high enough for it to be safe, though no one was sure of absolute recovery. I was sent home with a raft of instructions. I was not allowed to lift the baby; I had to stay in bed. I had to see all my doctors every other day. "Bring me Max," I urged, but when Jeff put him on my lap, his little arms reached for his father. We kept trying every day, and Max kept slapping me away.

In my vulnerable state, my insecurities flared. What kind of mother was I? What had I done to this child? And what had happened to my dream of how I was going to help raise him?

It was Jeff again who came to my rescue. "You just need more time together," he told me. This terrified me, because more time meant more screams. But as I got better, relearned how to walk, and got stronger, I began giving my son his bottle at night, and rocking him as he fed. I changed his diapers and talked to him, always in a low and soothing voice. I never asked for more than he would give me, and, believing that babies sense things, I never let him see me upset.

Instead, I shared my sorrows with Jeff, sobbing, "The baby doesn't love me."

Jeff said, "He will."

And then one day after feeding Max, I lay on the day bed in his room beside him. We faced one another and I began, once again, to talk gently to him, to tell him how I felt, how hard this was for me.

How none of this was his fault or my doing, and that I loved him right down to my bones. He yawned, and I thought he was disinterested. I was about to give up for the day. But then he put his hand, like a small starfish, against my cheek. I didn't move, didn't unlock my eyes from him, and he fell asleep in my arms.

And by the time Jeff got home, we were still that way, and I was smiling.

It got better after that. And I got better. When a year had passed, we began to take him places, to show him the world, to bind together more as a family. "Mommy, Mommy," he called for me. We hugged, kissed, and glue-bonded. I never for a second forgot how lucky I was to have survived, and to have had this chance to love my son.

Finally, I was told I didn't have to see all my doctors every week. I was told my condition had resolved, which is a fancy way of saying I would probably be OK. I began to see a cognitive therapist to talk about my guilt, my grief, and all that I had missed. Over time, I started to let it go. I stopped blaming myself about what had been taken from us all, and instead focused on the now—a loving family, a healthy baby! All of it was so worth any past pain.

My son is now twenty-four. He's an actor and a screenwriter, and he's handsome and sensitive and so, so kind. He remembers things we taught him when he was little, like that it didn't matter what he chose to do in life for work as long as he loved it. That being kind matters more than anything. My memories of that painful time have faded, replaced by the new ones we've made as a family. We are all so lucky.

And we have fun together. It was my son who convinced me to swim out to a waterfall with him in Hawaii even though I was terrified—and it turned out to be the best experience of my life. It made me feel brave! We go to virtual-reality places, too, and if there's a horror movie playing, it has our name on it. I asked him recently if there was any way I had failed him as a parent over the years. "Oh my God," he said, rolling his eyes. "I love you."

Caroline Leavitt is the *New York Times* bestselling author of twelve novels, including *Pictures of You, Cruel Beautiful World,* and *With or Without You.* She is a book critic for the *San Francisco Chronicle,* AARP, and *People.* A New York Foundation of the Arts Fellow, she was long-listed for the Maine Readers Prize, and was a finalist in the Sundance Screenwriters Lab. She teaches writing at both Stanford and the UCLA Writers Program online and works with private clients.

My Good Body

ELIZABETH LESSER

I did not grow up in a religious home. My parents were literature-loving, nature-revering atheists. But still, there were spoken and unspoken moral equations in the family that went something like this: $x + y$ = good person, where x is you, and y is a narrow range of how to act, speak, think, vote. One of the most potent equations was a remnant from my mother's childhood. Raised by devout Christian Scientist parents, my mother renounced the faith when she had her own kids, but she hung on to this bit of dogma: you + being sick = bad girl; you + being well = good girl.

Christian Scientists believe that the real identity of a human being is wholly spiritual, and therefore any feelings, longings, or sufferings that have to do with the body—vanity, sex, illness—are illusory and a sign of impure, incorrect thought. My mother might have left the church, but the church never left her. She still admonished me and my three sisters when we paid too much attention to what we looked like, or when we asked her about sex, or when we complained about feeling sick—from a sore throat to that time when I slipped running on the newly waxed floor and broke my arm. It took a lot of convincing that I wasn't exaggerating, that my arm really was twisted into an unnatural shape, and that perhaps I needed to go to the hospital. I wore my cast with both pride and shame. Pride, that indeed my body was real enough to deserve the kind of care the whole world could see. Shame, that there was something wrong with me—that my physical attention-seeking made me weak, shallow, sinful.

I was sick a lot as a kid—strep throat, ear infections, belly aches. My complaints were mostly ignored or met with accusations of hypochondria. I carried with me the nagging sense that focusing on my body for any reason, especially when it came to illness, was a useless, second-rate endeavor. Better to concentrate on the intellect, on creativity, or on social issues. Better to cultivate a stoic person's attitude toward pain and pleasure. Better to ignore the yearnings, and the fears, and the messages that began to pool in my body—as stress, as sadness, as confusion, and as mysterious aches and pains.

There's a line in James Joyce's book, *The Dubliners,* where he describes one of the characters as living "a short distance from his body." That's how my sisters and I went out into the world . . . living a short distance from our bodies. Kudos to our parents for teaching us to follow our minds into meaningful careers (which we did), and to listen to our consciences to do good in the world (a calling I still try to answer). But we had not been taught how to care for our precious bodies, or how to, as the poet Mary Oliver writes, "let the soft animal of the body love what it loves." It would take two things—my first career as a midwife and the demise of my marriage—to finally awaken my body and show it how to love what it loves.

When I was nineteen years old, I met the man who would become my first husband. At the time, I was in college and he was in medical school, and I became intrigued with the stories he told me about delivering babies. Which is what I ended up doing with him after we got married. Perhaps it was just luck, or maybe it was my way of rebelling (disembodied girl marries a doctor, becomes a midwife), but caring for pregnant women and delivering babies delivered me. Midwifery set me on the path to healing not only from my own misconceptions about the body, but also from the myths told from antiquity about the inferiority, the sinfulness, and the devious sexuality of the female form.

There I was, living "a short distance from my body," close up to the sacred, visceral, erotic process of birth. Every time a baby left the womb on its little hero's journey and was pushed into the world by its gallant mother, I felt an ache in me. At first it was an ache with no name. I'd leave a birth both exhilarated and wistful. A melancholy would settle in my heart. I thought maybe I could quell the sadness by having my own babies. And, in a roundabout way, that is exactly what happened. The primal experience of carrying life, the wild ride of labor and delivery, and the sensuality of nursing a baby, of smelling its skin, and feeling its warmth, gave me a name for the longing: *I wanted to live in my body*. To love it, to listen to it, to know that it was good—as good as the bodies of the babies I had carried and delivered and loved with all my heart.

Once I unlocked the longing and gave it a name (I called it my "good body") I had to listen to its messages; I had to follow its direction. At first the voice of my good body was tenuous—almost a whisper. Other voices in my head were louder: the voice of my mother; the voice of my fear of change; the voices of the ancient stories that have led women astray for millennia: Eve, Pandora, Cassandra, Hester Prynne, Rapunzel, and on and on. Women punished for being "born second, yet first to sin"; women called witches for following their intuition and instincts; women told to cover their nakedness lest it tempt men, all the while being sexualized, used, abused, confused.

The old stories have long tails. We are still under their sway. It took me a lot of inner work, a failed first marriage, and a rocky yet courageous midlife journey to step into the thing closest to me—my own body; my beloved chariot that carries me through life. And when I did, I recovered my health, my vibrant sexuality, and a sense of a home in the world wherever I go.

A few years ago, my sisters and I sat around my mother's bed for hours and hours as she struggled to leave the body she had never fully lived in. She had come to the end of a long, painful, unnecessary illness, one that she could have treated if she had not lived a short distance from her body. As she went in and out of consciousness, we held her hands. We stroked her feet. We kissed her face. We loved the body she had rejected; we told her it was good, that she was good. And after she died, we washed her body before it was taken away to be buried in the good earth. In caring for her in her last moments, we were also caring for ourselves. In loving her body, we were promising to love our own.

I still sometimes catch myself living a short distance from my body, denying its needs and longings and messages. But then I think of my mother and the pleasure and health she missed out on. And I think I hear a new voice—her voice—telling me that my body is good, that I am good.

Elizabeth Lesser is the author of several bestselling books, including *Cassandra Speaks* and *Broken Open*. She is the cofounder of the Omega Institute, recognized internationally for its workshops and conferences in wellness, spirituality, creativity, and social change. She is one of Oprah Winfrey's Super Soul 100, a collection of a hundred leaders who are using their voices and talent to elevate humanity.

A Son, Not My Own

GIGI LEVANGIE

My husband filed for divorce the day after I dressed up in a Dolce & Gabbana summery frock and told Matt Lauer on national television that our marriage was stronger than ever. *My bad.* He moved out and our two boys and I stayed in our secluded, gated Palisades estate where I was, ironically, terrified. We lived on three and a half acres with a security system that would scream if a gentle breeze blew. Where I came from, a dog and a baseball bat were a security system, and neither had let me down.

At bedtime, the kids and I huddled in my older boy's room. He and the three-year-old slept on the twin bed. I slept on the floor.

One night, the security alarm went off (again) at the witching hour. I called 911 while a bead of sweat wended its way down my spine. The police officers got lost navigating our winding pitch-black driveway. I could see by the looks on their faces that they thought it was crazy that anyone lived this way—three small people alone on a hill.

I needed help. I called Frankie, my twenty-one-year-old nephew, who was living in the loft apartment behind a home I owned in Venice. Frankie was a club promoter; he'd moved into the apartment after leaving the snowboarding boarding school I'd sent him to. Frankie was a beautiful boy, a Colombian-American mix, who was quick to find friends, girls, mischief, and an errant chess game. Within weeks of moving to Venice, he'd been surrounded by pals, a group of hardworking, hard-playing boys—directors, actors, writers.

He enjoyed a full, carefree life, playing competitive chess on Venice Beach, surfing with his buds, and spending hours filling his clubs with beautiful girls.

Frankie was the first "Levangie" baby. He had grown up in a bullet-ridden trailer with his younger brother and sister and his mother—my lovely, athletic, California blonde sister, who was an addict, a dealer, an entrepreneur of sorts, a person who transformed tubs of Sudafed for the Mexican mafia into a concoction that would leave you high, and, eventually, toothless and disheveled.

My nephew was born a miracle; my sister's ex-husband had shot her in the stomach at point-blank range; she was down to one Fallopian tube. My family and I decided that he was "our" baby—we'd all raise him.

My sister, the new baby, and I lived in my mother's house. I was working in "the" industry, developing shows for a television producer. I dressed in suits and heels ("borrowed" from my mother) and pretended that my life was as smooth and easy as the other young up-and-coming execs with their BMWs and credit cards. At night, when our new baby cried, I'd cradle Frankie in my arms and whisper in his tiny, perfectly formed ear a promise: I would take care of him, always.

Frankie was happy to stay with us in that estate on the hill, and my boys were ecstatic to have their cousin around. He moved into the guesthouse overlooking the Santa Monica Mountains. With Frankie came joy: back flips into the pool, barbecues, music, laughter, Guitar Hero. I became den mother to a group of twenty-something boys. We watched movies: Tom Cruise in *Jerry Maguire* (they knew every single word) and Daniel Day-Lewis in *There Will Be Blood* (about a thousand times). We talked about their ambitions, their regrets, their fears, who they wanted to "date" and who they wanted to marry.

We were, above all, a happy, functional home.

Frankie had a nagging eye infection and I pressed hot compresses on it. It went away, and then would reappear. Then his lower back started to hurt. I placed heating pads on his back, then ice. My ministrations gave him no relief. Finally, my doctor gave him a full check-up.

Frankie informed me that the doctor was concerned with one of his, er, testicles.

Really.

Yeah.

I breathed deeply, calming my fears. This kid had been through such a rough childhood—at five, climbing into cupboards to find cereal to feed his baby sister and brother; at seven, hiding when a SWAT team barreled through his mom's trailer, killing the blind Chow Chow who'd barked to warn his family.

There was no fucking way God would give this kid cancer.

Frankie went on a trip to Italy, where his best friend was promoting his movie. He would celebrate his twenty-second birthday overseas in grand style. The director, a famous actor who'd known him all of three weeks, ordered five cakes for him, with lit candles.

A few days after he returned, Frankie and I were in a small, sterile room with the doctor. I'd been in this room many times before, for yearly physicals, minor ailments.

"Testicular cancer," the doctor said.

I held onto the cabinet. Frankie was strong and still, unemotional, his brown eyes searching mine.

"But it's probably not the bad kind," the doctor continued.

A couple days later, we were told it was the bad kind.

The famous director who'd thrown Frankie his lavish birthday party called him after hearing about Frankie's diagnosis from his young star.

"This is un-fucking-acceptable!" the director said, "Stay by the phone. I'm having Lance Armstrong call you in five minutes."

Lance talked to Frankie for forty-five minutes, walking him

through the impending terror, step by horrible step. He, too, had had the "bad kind."

"By the third week," Lance had said, "you'll feel like killing yourself. But you will survive. You will get through this."

He made Frankie promise to call him whenever he needed to.

The cancer was fast moving; a few days later, Frankie had an operation to remove his faulty testicle. His friends immediately started calling him "The Uni-Baller." Of course.

Frankie would only listen to classical music in the car on the way to the oncology center. Only classical would do. I remember his mother playing the piano, my grandmother's old upright, in the trailer—sitting there for hours, her fingers dancing across the keys, conjuring a different sort of high.

As his treatment intensified, Frankie's long, shiny brown locks withered. Finally, he shaved it all off. His friends shaved their own heads, in unity. He had to wear adult diapers; my three-year-old would snuggle next to him in bed, a pacifier in his mouth. "Frankie's my baby," he'd say, rubbing his head.

Frankie's nausea became unbearable; the prescription meds were useless. Desperate, I called around to find marijuana. Frankie didn't want to smoke, rejecting my "gift." The child of a drug dealer wouldn't smoke—until I did.

Frankie's body was brutalized after the second round of chemo, which had lasted all day long for five days. Saturday night, we were back at Cedars-Sinai, in the emergency room. Frankie yelled out in pain. A baby howled in the background. The place was crowded with patients.

Frankie was ripping the catheter out of his arm. I was helpless. I had lied; I couldn't take care of my baby.

At the house, Guitar Hero was played less and less.

When Frankie went into the third and final round of chemo, he rebelled. "I can't do it," he told the burly Hispanic male nurse. "I'm not going to do it."

We begged him. He had a spot on his lung, a shadow on his liver. The nurse spelled out the reality for him: *You will die,* he told him. *You will die unless you get chemo.*

Finally, Frankie relented. He barely made it through that following weekend. We almost lost him, again, this time to a nurse's near-overdose of pain medication.

And then, just like that, the cancer was gone. We could breathe again. Frankie started recovering, peach fuzz appearing on his head.

One day, I found myself crying, alone, in my kitchen, where I'd been chopping vegetables for dinner. I couldn't stop.

Frankie hobbled up, still weak from treatment, and put his arms around me. My son, not my own, held me while I sobbed. Twenty-two years had passed since I had whispered in this baby's ear, the first baby among four sisters. *I will take care of you.*

I told my boy, through my tears, "Thank you for taking care of us."

Now, I think back fondly to those nights when the alarm would go off. Signaling that something was wrong. Something was terribly wrong.

That Christmas, I gave Frankie the gift of a new, state-of-the-art ball. He now has a full set.

Gigi Levangie is the author of several novels including *The Starter Wife,* which was adapted as an Emmy-winning miniseries, and *Maneater,* which was adapted for a Lifetime miniseries. Her latest novel is *Been There, Married That.* She also wrote the screenplay for the movie *Stepmom* with Julia Roberts and Susan Sarandon. Her articles have appeared in *Vogue, Harper's Bazaar,* and *Glamour.* She currently lives in Los Angeles.

My Father Immortal

EMILY LIEBERT

I sat on the bleachers next to my parents, watching my seven-year-old son Hugo's Little League game. It was a Sunday morning in September and we chatted about everything and nothing: standard fare for our family.

As Hugo stepped up to bat, our conversation quieted. He was the smallest one on the team but a robust athlete, much like my father.

The pitcher, a tall angular boy with a gummy grin, hurled the ball toward home plate.

Strike one. I cleared my throat and shifted in my seat. The pitcher wound up again.

Strike two. My mother and I exchanged an anxious glance as my dad approached the fence to get a closer look, revealing his competitive nature.

The pitcher flung the ball at the catcher once more, and with the crack of his bat, Hugo hit a line drive down the center, affording him a well-deserved single. I exhaled and glanced at my father standing ten feet away. But it wasn't the expression of pride on his face that struck me. It was the way his hand was trembling at his side, an unmistakable tremor that appeared beyond his control.

I turned to my mother. "What's going on with that?" I asked, motioning to my father's hand.

"Oh, yeah, Daddy has Parkinson's," she replied.

I laughed. "What are you talking about?"

Obviously she was mistaken. If my father had a *disease*, clearly I would know about it. Clearly *someone* would have informed me of this seemingly critical information. And *not* on the sideline of my son's baseball game on a sunny September morning where nothing could go wrong.

"He's had it for about six years." She nodded.

My internal voice grasped at sarcasm: *Oh, okay. Six years. Well that makes sense. So just a little half-dozen-year secret. No big deal. I'm cool.*

As my father approached us, my eyes flooded with tears.

"I told Emily about your Parkinson's," my mom said.

I waited for a denial. *Come on, Dad. Tell her she must be confused. It's just arthritis, maybe dehydration. Go ahead. I'm ready.*

But he didn't say anything.

We just sat in silence for the next two innings until the game was over.

I drove home with Hugo peppering me with baseball trivia from the back seat of my car as my parents followed behind us. The constant refrain—*My father has Parkinson's disease*—repeated in my head like a stuttering record.

I pulled into the driveway, burst into our house, ran up the stairs, and collapsed onto my bed in a fit of self-pity and despair, leaving Hugo to unload his equipment from the trunk, blissfully unaware of the pretext for my quick getaway.

Questions fired in all corners of my brain: *Why my dad? Why now? Why didn't I see it? Why didn't anyone tell me?*

My husband would later admit that he'd suspected it for a long time. Resentment simmered inside: *Why hadn't he said anything? Why was everyone treating me like a child?*

Growing up, we're meant to believe that our parents are immortal. What's fascinating about this particular belief is that, in most cases, there's ample evidence to the contrary. I had a close friend who lost her mother when we were fifteen years old. There was also a boy in my elementary school class whose father died by suicide, inhaling carbon monoxide in their garage.

Still, for whatever reason, I assumed that nothing bad would happen to anyone in my family. I was born with all four grandparents, three of whom lived until I was an adult, and the fourth is ninety-seven years young! I even had a great-grandparent who survived until I was seventeen. Of course, now that I'm forty-four with two children of my own, I realize how rare all of that is.

My father has always been a pillar of strength—mentally, emotionally, and physically. He's a triathlete. He ran a sixty-two-mile marathon in Poland. But, more than that, he's a healer, a world-renowned surgeon. He *helps* sick people. He fixes them. He *does not* get sick himself.

Except that now he has Parkinson's disease, a condition with no cure. It sometimes feels impossible to hold those two truths at once, but each day I try. My father's strength and his vulnerability are now inextricably linked.

This juxtaposition couldn't have been clearer than when I endured my own health scare in 2020. While the world was fixated on combating a terrifying virus called COVID-19, I was fighting a private battle of my own: The reality that, as a healthy mother of two in her forties, my kidneys might be failing me. It took five months of endless doctors' visits, bottomless blood tests, and two procedures to figure out that my kidneys are, in fact, in good shape. But, in that nearly half-year period of time, there were too many sleepless nights, too many tears, and too many unanswered questions. *Would I have to go on dialysis? Would I need a kidney transplant? Would I be able to live a full life and watch my kids grow into adults?*

My father held my hand every step of the way. He was there for me every time I called crying. He spoke to my doctors directly so he could arm himself with as much information as possible. He knew how scared I was. And I knew how scared he was, even more for me than for himself.

Although he couldn't be there when I had my kidney biopsy

(again, COVID-19), he spoke to me on the phone immediately before and after. Lying in that hospital bed, listening to my dad's voice, I couldn't help but reflect on his lifelong support and how that child-like reverence for our parents, and the desire for them to comfort us, never goes away, even as they age and we age and the caregiving relationship is reversed.

"You can do this, Em," he said, reassuring me that—whatever the outcome—we would figure it out together.

It was exactly what I needed to hear.

Emily Liebert is the *USA Today* bestselling author of seven books including *Pretty Revenge* and *Perfectly Famous*. Her work has been featured in media outlets like *The Rachael Ray Show*, *Anderson Cooper 360°*, FOX News, the *New York Times*, the *Wall Street Journal*, and the *Chicago Tribune*. Emily lives with her husband, Lewis, and their two sons, Jax and Hugo, in Westport, CT, and Miami, FL.

Click, Click, Click Through My Mind

ZIBBY OWENS

At first, I just couldn't find the right words. I would open my mouth to speak and my brain would spin in circles like an unwanted rainbow swirl on a frozen computer.

"It's in the garbage," I would answer, when asked the whereabouts of something in the garage.

People's names? Forget it. I would pass women about my age, then my early thirties, on the street and they would stop and say, "Zibby!" We would chitchat and part ways. Meanwhile, I couldn't remember who they were or how I knew them.

I even started getting lost. On the way back from running to a drugstore down the block, I suddenly stopped on the street I'd traversed a million times and couldn't remember where I was or which direction would take me home. I just froze on that tree-lined New York City street, cars whizzing past, clutching a white plastic shopping bag, and knew that the cognitive impairment I'd noticed was getting worse. I called my (now ex) husband and said I felt like I was losing my mind. He stayed on the phone until I could get my bearings.

Admittedly, it was a stressful time. I had three-and-a-half-year-old twins in the "terrible threes" who didn't sleep. At all. We were in a temporary rental apartment with none of our creature comforts while our home was being renovated. The loving nanny on whom I depended, whom I loved like a best friend, whose former boyfriend I'd helped catch having an affair, suddenly left our family—and New

York—after a cancer diagnosis. (She is now fine, but never came back to work.) I wasn't getting along with my husband. I was out of sorts, depressed, and a bit lost emotionally from not working after decades of academic and professional rigor.

"I think I'm losing my mind," I confessed to some fellow moms while sitting on plastic folding chairs, watching an indoor Kids in Sports gym class through glass doors. "I can't even form proper sentences anymore."

"Mom brain," one friend responded, waving her hand dismissively.

"Me too," another said.

"Totally," another added.

"It happens to everyone," a wiser mom with older kids advised.

I tried not to worry. But eventually I consulted a doctor who referred me to a neurologist. Suddenly, I was sitting in a wood-paneled waiting room with white-haired octogenarians who shuffled into the exam rooms ahead of me. What was I doing? The neurologist kindly examined me and then ordered a bunch of tests. I went from kids' music classes to having little plastic nodes glued onto my head to assess my brain function; reading *Goodnight Moon* to sitting in hospital hallways waiting for full-body MRIs. I even endured a ten-hour, multi-step neuro-psychological assessment.

And I did it all alone, accompanied only by fear. My mom friends said it was par for the course. But I just knew something was off.

As I paced in the rental apartment one afternoon trying unsuccessfully to get the kids to take naps, the doctor called.

"We found some abnormalities on the MRI," he said quickly. "Looks like a cyst of some type on your brain. Probably nothing to worry about. Not sure if it's causing the memory problems. Don't think it's malignant. Probably benign, but I'll get back to you when I know more."

"Sorry, wait," I said, grabbing a pen and paper. "Could you say that again?"

I had what was soon identified as a colloid cyst (5 mm) in the third ventricle of my brain. I'd had bouts with headaches years earlier so I had an older MRI to compare this one to. The neurologist read the report and decided the tumor had been growing rapidly. Brain surgery was quickly on the table.

I told my family and some close girlfriends, who all helped me get other opinions. I sent my MRI results to hospitals all over the country. Every single surgeon I spoke to recommended immediate surgery as a preventative measure. If I waited, the tumor could maintain its quick rate of growth and start having a real, negative impact.

Suddenly I was juggling whether a surgeon should go in through the top of my skull or if they could do it non-invasively. Meanwhile, I was managing the move into our new home, the ever-present needs of two wildly different twins, and the rest of life. And I still couldn't keep anything straight in my head. I overate to dull the feelings, getting to the point where all I could wear was leggings with long, billowy sweaters, which I wrapped tightly around me.

On my sixth opinion, one I almost didn't even get, I met a white-haired, spry neurologist who decided to analyze the hundreds of different slides and slices from my original MRIs years earlier, which hadn't shown a mass at all. Unlike the other doctors, he didn't take the radiologist's report at face value. I sat across the giant wooden desk from him, sun pouring in through the window, fractured by white, slatted blinds, as he leaned forward toward his computer, slowly studying the images of my brain, pre-tumor. I couldn't even breathe. I just watched him click, click, click through my mind.

And then he stopped clicking. "A-ha! There it is!" he exclaimed. He turned around the screen and, in the shadows of the images, there was the same "new" tumor, now not new at all.

"It's probably been there your whole life," he said, studying the image again and toggling between two slides that clearly showed it. "It doesn't need to come out. It hasn't even grown. Same size. Probably just a benign colloid cyst. Very common."

"You're 100 percent sure?" I asked.

"100 percent. You can see it yourself," he said.

And I could.

Had I not seen this doctor, the last stop on my multi-opinion tour, I would've had a variety of eager-to-operate surgeons claw into my head, perhaps destroying what made me *me*.

"What about my memory loss? My cognitive impairment?"

He looked at me with sad, sympathetic eyes. Really seeing me.

"It's probably stress and sleep-deprivation. Get some rest. You're going to be fine."

I could barely stand up, flooded by relief.

It's ten years later, and the cyst is still there. It hasn't grown, as my annual MRIs show—when I remember to get them. I still lose my ability to retrieve words when I'm extremely tired. Sometimes I don't recognize friends on the street who clearly know me. I occasionally get lost and disoriented, but my neuropsych test results reflected my already-known "impaired" visual-spatial abilities, so compromised that I can literally get lost in my own neighborhood.

My twins are now teenagers and one of them sleeps later than me, although I ended up having two more children who still sneak in at night. I got divorced and then remarried. The home we renovated was sold years ago. My "new" husband comes with me to every single doctor's appointment and holds my hand in the waiting room. I never even have to ask. My brain remains untouched, thanks to that one doctor who took a little extra time for me. If only I could remember his name to thank him.

Zibby Owens is the creator and host of the award-winning podcast *Moms Don't Have Time to Read Books.* She is a regular contributor to *Good Morning America* online and the *Washington Post,* and her work has appeared in *Real Simple, Parents, Marie Claire, Redbook,* and many other publications. She lives in New York with her husband, Kyle, and her four children.

Nana's Last Ride

ELIZABETH PASSARELLA

I was no one's first choice to chauffeur my grandmother from Ripley, Mississippi, to Little Rock. But one day when I was home for spring break during my freshman year of college, my mother woke me up with the announcement that I needed to drive to my grandmother's house ASAP. It was 1996.

My grandmother Frances, whom we called Nana, lived alone in Ripley, a small town less than two hours southeast of my hometown of Memphis. Apparently, Nana's sister, Woody, who lived next door, had called my mother and ominously declared, "Somethin's wrong with Fanny. Y'all gotta come see about her." In addition to several friends from Nana's bridge group expressing concern at her erratic play, Woody said, the home health aide who had recently been hired found Nana hiding in the closet when she arrived that morning.

Having never experienced dementia, I can only imagine that it sneaks up on you. It sneaks up on the people around you too. Nana was a workhorse, always awake early to make biscuits or tend to her garden. She was tough and spirited and good at masking any confusion or forgetfulness on the phone. She reluctantly accepted limited help from the home health aide, only because my mother and all three of her siblings lived out of state. Everyone was still sure she was fine in her own house, especially with her sister next door. (Note: A few years later, Woody began to insist that there were aliens living in her ceiling, proof that all of the women in our family should be working extra crossword puzzles.)

The realization that Nana's situation had gone farther south than we'd realized prompted quick action. My mother's brother, Max, and his wife, Patti, found an in-patient dementia clinic in Little Rock, where they lived. There was one available spot, the clinic informed Max, but Nana would need to be there by the next day.

The trip seemed perilous for a few reasons: One, we weren't crystal clear on what I'd be walking into at Nana's house. Two, I was a terrible driver. With a broken sense of direction and a tendency to have distracting, imaginary conversations while behind the wheel, I'd managed to hit mailboxes, ding bumpers, and, once, I even broadsided a tour bus. But my parents were both working, and my older sister no longer lived at home. The trip couldn't wait. I was the only option.

I don't remember much about picking up Nana from her house. She was happy to see me as she climbed into the front seat of my Honda Accord with her purse and medicine case, a rounded leather cube the size and weight of a car battery that had stackable trays filled with everything from Alka Seltzer to surgical gauze. Her hair was a faded, rusty pink, the closest she ever got to her original auburn, and she smelled strongly of Clinique Dramatically Different Moisturizer. "Well, hello," she said, and then let out a deep chuckle and waved to the aide as I backed away from the plain brick house my grandfather built in 1963. She'd never live there again.

My goal was to make it to Little Rock before dark, but by the time we crossed the Mississippi River into Arkansas, it was pouring, and I knew my limitations. Slowing to the pace of a tractor and trying to stay in line with the fuzzy brake lights ahead of me, my thoughts ranged from terrified to indignant. Who had put me in charge, anyway? I was barely nineteen. I wanted Nana to drive. I wanted someone else to handle this.

"I think I'd like to stop and get me something to eat," Nana said.

I pulled into the first restaurant I saw: an Arby's. After walking slowly across the parking lot under a shared umbrella, we both headed for the restroom. There were two stalls, and after a minute or two, I saw a puddle forming on the floor next to me.

"Nana? You OK?"

"Hoo boy. I've missed the toilet."

I told her to stay put, and I ran back to the car, popping open her suitcase and grabbing clean pants. Back in the restroom, I squeezed into the stall, wrapping my arms around her soft torso to lift her up so she could step out of her old elastic-waist, polyester pants and into the fresh ones.

At our table, Nana ate a few bites of her chicken sandwich, then began to wrap up everything that wasn't yet finished and furtively tuck the items in her purse. I took that as a sign we should get back on the road. Less than an hour later, Nana removed her dentures. She'd had all her teeth pulled years before and wore a full, fake top and bottom set which sat in a short glass of bubbling Polident by her bathroom sink every night, freaking out whichever grandchild came eye to eye with them during a 2 a.m. toilet run. She began to fish through her medicine case, and when I looked over she was squeezing a thick, white line of hemorrhoid cream onto the surface of her dentures, mistaking it for Fixodent.

"Nana! No!" I screamed, jerking the car wheel and flying onto the shoulder. I knocked the dentures out of her hands just as she was opening wide to slide them back in.

We made it to Max and Patti's house in Little Rock well after dark. I sat at their kitchen counter, emptying the half-eaten Arby's food out of Nana's purse while recounting the rain, the bathroom accident, the hemorrhoid cream. The next day, I hugged Nana good-bye in the narrow back hallway of my aunt and uncle's house, then slipped into the garage and out to the driveway, relieved that she was safe and no longer my responsibility. I drove home to resume my spring break. I didn't—couldn't—appreciate that it was the most lucid and familiar she'd ever be to me again.

Nana went to the dementia clinic for a time, and then lived with Max and Patti and their three young children for a couple of years before moving into a nursing home near my mom in Memphis, where she died in 1999.

I am now forty-four and the mother of three children. I'm still a bad driver; I rear-ended someone just last week. But I am a pretty good caretaker. That rainy car trip with Nana was a slow peeling back of expectations, and of innocence, for me. Within five or six hours, I went from the kid who was looking forward to a free fast-food combo meal from her grandmother to the grownup responsible for the safety and comfort of another human.

At this point in my life, I've changed more than my share of elastic-waist pants in public restrooms and cleaned up countless toilet accidents. I've knocked dangerous substances out of my children's hands in the nick of time. Nana never met any of my kids, but she certainly prepared me for them. She spent years serving her loved ones in challenging, often messy, circumstances—and she spent one long day, whether she remembered or not, letting me do the same.

Elizabeth Passarella is a magazine writer and author of the essay collection *Good Apple: Tales of a Southern Evangelical in New York*. She lives in New York City with her family.

The S Word

SUSIE ORMAN SCHNALL

Sometimes I can be a real gem. Like when I ask my husband to change the channel, quickly, because I can't absorb all the sadness of the news. Or when I have to relocate my yoga mat because whatever perfume you're wearing will most certainly be too much for me to handle for the next hour.

I've always tried to be more tolerant. More laid back. Less reactive. Not so damn *sensitive.*

For me, being sensitive has always been a burden. *You're so sensitive* has never been said to me in a kind tone. It's always been an accusation, a criticism, a taunt: *Don't get emotional. Don't overanalyze everything. Don't ask them to turn down the music.* Don't be who you just can't help being—you're making everyone else uncomfortable.

Sure, I have friends who cry while watching poignant commercials. Friends who feel overwhelmed when there are too many piles, too many to-dos, too many people needing/calling/asking. But I always sensed that the way I coped with those same situations was just more heightened. There was a certain intensity and debilitating aspect for me that I never saw in others.

When I was younger, I assumed everyone felt the same way. I didn't have the tools to delve deeply into my friends' processing systems. I didn't think to ask how they synthesized information, how their brains reacted to stimuli. Our conversations centered around which flavor Bonne Bell Lip Smacker was better or whether they were bringing their roller skates to the sleepover.

But as I got older, I realized I was different. What I would later learn is a superpower felt for years like a personality flaw, a tremendous shortcoming, something to be embarrassed by and ashamed of.

Last year, those feelings began to shift after I came upon a website that changed everything.

I was sitting alone in my office late one night—it's where I do my best writing and sleuthing. Googling my "symptoms" was a regular affair for me; I don't recall whether my search was "Why do I startle so easily?" or "Extreme sensitivity to smells and noises," or one of the many other frustrating aspects of being me. But suddenly there it was, a blog post from a site I had never noticed before: hsperson.com—The Highly Sensitive Person.

As I clicked around the sedate green and white site—probably designed *not* to overstimulate—I felt a low thrum of excitement in my stomach. It was like finally finding the treasure chest and knowing there's something good inside even though you have no idea what it will be.

The copy on the homepage called out to me like a carnival barker. "Is this you?" What followed was a list of eight characteristics. Uh-huh. Yes. That's me. Oh my God! And then a link to take a quiz.

The questions were simple enough: Do other people's moods affect you? Are you particularly sensitive to the effects of caffeine? Are you bothered by intense stimuli, like loud noises or chaotic scenes? As I made my way through, clicking "agree" to more and more boxes, tears began to fill my eyes.

I felt truly seen for perhaps the first time in my life.

I clicked "finish" and expected one of those pages that asks for $99.99 to access your results. Instead, I got my score straightaway: "If you answered more than fourteen of the questions as true of yourself," said the quiz, "you are probably highly sensitive." I had scored twenty-five out of twenty-seven.

I spent the next hour reading through everything on the site, and

I felt like I was seeing the blueprint of my entire being. I learned that there is an innate trait called Sensory Processing Sensitivity (SPS), and a person with SPS is known as a Highly Sensitive Person (HSP). I discovered psychologist Dr. Elaine Aron, who created hsperson.com, and has been researching "high sensitivity" for thirty years.

Instead of feeling anxious about my internet self-diagnosis, I felt elated. I felt validated. I wasn't too weak, too difficult, too fragile. I was sensitive, goddammit, and that was perfectly fine. It was, in fact, good!

My research on HSP life picked up in the following weeks and months. According to Dr. Aron, because of the way HSPs' brains process information, they tend to become more easily overwhelmed and startled. She writes "[HSPs] have unusual empathy . . . They also have more active 'mirror neurons' in the brain, so sometimes it is almost as though what someone else feels is what they are feeling."

On the plus side, HSPs are known to have a rich inner life, to be extremely intuitive and empathetic, to find the beauty in small things.

Since learning about SPS, I've come to wear my acronym like a badge of honor. I no longer beat myself up for feeling all the feelings, for retreating out of loud stores, or for not wanting to go to a concert, which I know will be too chaotic for my comfort level. And I feel grateful for my SPS when I know it's responsible for an empathetic and appreciated reaction to others' plights or for the tears that fill my eyes during a particularly glorious sunrise.

There is no "cure" for SPS, although sometimes I wish there were. It would make it easier to go through this life of ours. Instead, there are only survival tips: get enough sleep, limit caffeine, give yourself breaks, blah, blah, blah. Basically, all the things that everyone should do for a healthy lifestyle.

So here I am. Off the charts HSP. Living in our highly sensory, overwhelming, turbulent world. I can't change that world, but I can adjust how I function inside of it. Sometimes I write "breathe" in Sharpie on my inner wrist. Sometimes I embark on a news fast. And sometimes I just find one of those particularly glorious sunrises and cry.

Susie Orman Schnall is the author of four novels: *We Came Here to Shine, The Subway Girls, The Balance Project,* and *On Grace*—and she also writes for print, television, and film. Schnall grew up in Los Angeles and now lives in New York with her husband and three sons.

Sunlight, Through an Angled Window

MELISSA T. SHULTZ

It was night when I found my lump. At the age of forty-five, with two young sons, the world of beginnings I'd just settled into felt as if it had skipped right to the end.

I was told it was slow-growing and treatable—a *good cancer*. But I didn't think the words *good* and *cancer* belonged in the same sentence; *good* belonged with grades, or cookies, or a job well done. My cancer was all-encompassing. It needed no descriptor.

When the surgery was over, my breasts, once the sole source of nourishment for my children, looked and felt as if they were marked by Zorro's sword. Both were cut and stitched, protected by gauze and stuffed into a contraption that bound them. They ached more than I thought possible. My mother flew in for a few days to help with my children, but found herself sitting in a chair she'd propped by the side of my bed, repeatedly stroking my middle-aged forehead with her withered, out-of-practice hands.

Though lumps on both breasts were removed, the biopsies revealed cancer in only the left. The tumor was small, so the doctor told me the choice to undergo chemotherapy was mine to make. A test through a free pilot program offered statistics to help in decision-making: The chances of a recurrence after surgery, radiation, and five years on the estrogen-blocking drug, Tamoxifen, were low. I took a leap of faith and opted against it.

Radiation offered a surprising sense of renewal, a literal beam of light to bring me out of the darkness that had set in since the diagnosis. While I sat in the waiting room of the cancer center, surrounded by survivors, sunlight streamed through angled windows and touched my face. Each weekday morning I changed into a hospital gown then lay on the treatment table beneath the massive radiation machinery. Tattooed marks on my chest served as a guide for the technician, a large burly man who had just lost his only son in a car accident, yet somehow still had enough compassion left over to ease my worries. "Everything is going to be OK," he'd tell me in his deep voice. I took this daily affirmation as a sign that I was regaining some control over what seemed like an uncontrollable, possibly life-ending event.

On his cue, I would lift both arms above my head and grab the handles behind me, exposing the nodes to be treated. Then he would move me into position. My focus was the tiny black box on the ceiling with red lights, and my mantra was *chocolate.*

He would then slide a cartridge into place to my right. To keep my skin from burning, he'd put a cardboard tampon applicator where the fold of my breast and chest wall met. Every time he did this I thought about the countless times I'd used them over my lifetime, never once imagining they'd eventually come to protect me from radiation beams on an entirely different part of my body.

Once the applicator was secure, I was cautioned not to move. The technician would close the treatment room door, locking me and the radiation inside. Just before the buzzer sounded, I'd shut my eyes and picture the two pieces of milk chocolate I'd leave each day on the kitchen table at home. They were truffles of the grocery-store variety, but luscious and beautiful nonetheless—eating them was a marker of another treatment crossed off my list.

And so it went. Fridays I got an X-ray, Tuesdays I saw the doctor. Saturdays and Sundays I was off.

The process was repeated over thirty-three weekdays. It was my job, along with my real job and being a mother—my *raison d'etre* from the moment I learned I was pregnant with each of my children.

A month or so after the last treatment, while my skin was still healing from radiation burns (despite those versatile tampon applicators), I swallowed the first of what would eventually be 1,825 doses of Tamoxifen taken over the next five years. From the very first pill, it became clear to me that the only obstacle standing in the way of a healthy future was my own perspective. I knew that studies showed that the level of optimism someone has can predict how well they recover from breast cancer treatment. I'd had surgery and radiation to eradicate the cancer, yet I wasn't allowing myself to believe it was gone. My body might betray me again, after all.

When I'd been diagnosed and heard the word *cancer,* I also heard the words *bad, ending,* and *death*. Not because anyone used them—they didn't—but because I imagined the worst before giving myself a chance to imagine the best. Every story I'd ever read about a mother with breast cancer seemed to end with their passing.

The idea of leaving my children without a mom, and not being able to watch them grow up—it was simply too much to wrap my head around all at once. Looking at a calendar and planning ahead felt impossible. But as the months passed, my perspective shifted, and my determination to be okay intensified. I began to exercise again, regain some of my strength and mobility, think about the future, and gravitate toward sunlight—on a walk, in a room, in my car. The warmth filled me with hope, and life began to feel more like a continuum. Not just a series of beginnings when everything seems possible, or endings, when everything comes to a close, but a series of middles. The middle is the part of life you work through. The middle is unfinished. Cancer became one of those middles.

I found the concept to be liberating. It was like the middle of a book, where the heart of the story lives. As a reader you're invested because there is still so much to learn—anything can happen. False endings along the way often alarm us before turning in a completely unexpected direction.

It's been fifteen years since my diagnosis, and the lessons of cancer continue to reveal themselves. Last week, for example, I showed up to get my COVID-19 vaccine. I got so close I could see the paperwork with my name on it. But there was confusion about my eligibility and I was unfortunately turned away. So I did what I've learned to do: I told myself that when I reach what seems to be a bad ending—and there have been many—I can choose to make it a middle instead, a middle filled with possibilities.

Melissa T. Shultz is a writer and editor whose work has been published by the *New York Times*, the *Washington Post*, the *Dallas Morning News*, AARP's *The Ethel*, and many other publications. She is editor-at-large for Jim Donovan Literary, and her memoir/self-help book *From Mom to Me Again* was named one of "Three Inspiring Reads" by Parade.com. Her first children's book is forthcoming from Familius.

MOMS
DON'T HAVE
TIME TO
SEE FRIENDS

We Met Online

CHANDLER BAKER

I joined my first online message board in 2008. Twenty-two-year-old me wanted to be a writer so badly it made my stomach literally hurt, and since I didn't know anyone else with my particular brand of—how shall I put it—enthusiasm, I opted to comb the corners of the internet.

I started with a forum thread called "Purgatory" on the Absolute Write message boards. There, I met a motley crew of wannabe writers who were keeping company during the stressful limbo of waiting to hear back from literary agents and editors. To the detriment of my grades, I spent a good portion of my first-year law-school classes hitting "refresh" on those pages, anxious to be included in the conversation. When I got my first offer of representation from a bona fide agent, I told the board first. When my boyfriend of five years dumped me unceremoniously, I told them that, too.

Eventually, my relationships in Purgatory started to get more serious and we were ready to "take things to the next level." Basically, we wanted to be able to do what all good friends do: tell secrets. And a publicly available forum wasn't cutting it anymore. So we started a listserv called The Hopefuls where we continued to share less censored versions of our long, winding journeys to publication.

I quickly developed a pretty full social life online. It's where I made my first online frenemy, when a woman told me on our *group* email chain "not to worry" because I was just a "casual writer" while the other writers in the group were "serious ones." I still don't know what that means, but ten years later I thought of her words when my first adult novel hit the *New York Times* bestseller list.

Back to my friends, though.

The Hopefuls died a slow, belabored death, but I found two women there with whom I talked on Gchat throughout every weekday, just like real, live co-workers.

While I had plenty of friends offline, my writing world got lonely, and the amount of rejection I was receiving from editors at the time was downright depressing. These two women kept me afloat. They held my hand—still virtually, but nevertheless. We formed a trio of support, gave advice on boyfriends, birth control, and job offers. Then, one of the women (let's call her Phantom Phoebe) . . . ghosted us. *Poof!* Mid-email chain she ceased all communication. (Side note, lest anyone be too concerned: We did worry that she was, in fact, dead and thus a ghost, but no, she's still active on Facebook. Crisis averted.) To this day, we've been haunted by the memory of Phantom Phoebe. Our leading theory is that she broke up with us because she no longer wanted to be an author and the sting of constant rejection proved too much. Which, OK, fine! Understandable! But the thing is: I thought our relationship had moved beyond just an online writing friendship. Had I been confusing virtual reality with reality-reality all along?

Phantom Phoebe had no ties to the rest of my life and so it was easy for her to disappear from it entirely. We would never bump into one another at a mutual friend's baby shower or have to stammer awkward hellos at the grocery store. But the loss of her still shook me.

With my social group depleted, I actively set out to make more friends, but as most grown-ups know, making friends as an adult is really freaking hard.

I still don't know what alchemy brought Charlotte and me together. One day I was culling through the hundreds of comments left by people looking for critique partners over on a popular agent's blog when I saw her post and reached out. For the past seven years, we have emailed each other once in the morning and once in the evening, Monday through Friday. We discuss our writing goals, yes, but also parenting decisions, exercise, life stresses, and other minutiae.

Charlotte and I sold our debut novels the same year, and like two kids starting at a brand new school, we sent our book babies out into the world together. We met other women who had debut books published the same year and our networks expanded.

For a long time, I made a distinction between my friends in "real life" and my "online friends," but not anymore. The lines have blurred too much. When, a couple years ago, my husband wanted to surprise me with a trip to Las Vegas for my birthday, it was Charlotte and her husband whom he called to join us.

As a matter of fact, I'm writing this essay during a virtual coffee shop date with my internet friends—a thing we started doing twice a week during the pandemic. We meet on Google Hangout to socialize and write for an hour and a half on Tuesdays and Thursdays.

For my friendships that started offline, the COVID-19 lockdown has been a stressor. We tend to feel disconnected when we don't see one another in person. But my internet friends? We're made for this.

Chandler Baker is the *New York Times* bestselling author of *The Husbands* and *Whisper Network,* a Reese Witherspoon book club selection. She lives in Austin, Texas, with her husband and two small children.

One on One
ADRIENNE BANKERT

Like many young broadcasters, I stubbornly held to a certain picture of success. I imagined it like this: On any given day, I would be researching late-breaking details as my producer frantically handed me a script. Feverishly tweaking each line, I'd deliver every phrase flawlessly as the camera rolled.

Well, it happened—I became a local news anchor. I loved the adrenaline rush and the potential to reach so many people at once. Little did I know that juggling stories and intense deadlines was teaching me an unexpected lesson: how to treat my crew, my family, and everyone with kindness—even while under immense pressure.

Confidence came as I shared others' stories. And I realized that to truly connect with an audience, I first needed to understand how to connect with just *one* person. Writing was key to helping me do that. Over time, writing allowed me to be more aware of others, to learn how to vibe and collaborate with my producers, and I began to embrace myself as a story originator.

A few years later, I was asked to volunteer for a community newspaper. I wrote secretly under an alias about mom-and-pop businesses, quaint towns, and quirky neighbors. Friends asked me to copyedit their books and draft press releases for their events. My news director assigned me to write more, particularly feature pieces about health and community.

All of this prepared me for a lifelong dream: working as a national correspondent for ABC News. Writing opened the door to other meant-to-be goals. I wrote my first book, *Your Hidden Superpower*, which led to speaking engagements, my own e-courses, and appearing in publications like *American Way* magazine. I put my ideas on paper during every waking moment between screens (YouTube, Facebook, Instagram Live, and Zoom). I would write on a flight to Tokyo to chat with Ryan Reynolds about his new movie, on red carpets in Los Angeles, and in my downtime while in Prague for an interview with Mark Hamill.

Staying creatively focused on storytelling also helped me be more open. I learned how to better express myself and practice more empathy. I carried those skills to shows like *Good Morning America* and *World News Tonight* and into my everyday life off-camera.

One morning in downtown Manhattan, as I was rushing to an appointment, I heard a baby cry, a blood curdling and painful wailing I could not ignore. Turning to the sound, I noticed a mother across the busy intersection. I quickly ran over and gave her some encouragement. I approached with a smile and looked into her wearied face as she held tightly to the stroller.

"Hi! How are you? I heard your baby girl all the way across the street!" I said. "My mom raised seven of us, mostly alone. It was hard sometimes. I just want to tell you it's going to be OK. You're going to have a great day," as I reached for an Altoids mint container in my purse, shaking it noisily in hopes of quieting her daughter.

"Oh my goodness, thank you," she said. "She has eczema so bad and is in constant pain. We've tried different ointments and I don't know what to do."

We talked for a few minutes. Amazingly, she also worked in broadcasting. We exchanged numbers and met for lunch a month later. The next year, she invited me to speak on a panel for one of the top *Fortune* 500 companies in the world.

My friend and I would have never met if I hadn't been curious and open to embracing the moment. In my day-to-day, I've noticed that when we're genuinely interested, we can see and seize opportunities. The practice allows new chapters to unfold.

It happens all the time. Before covering the Academy Awards in 2020, I was seated in a nail salon getting a manicure next to a woman with a warm smile and kind eyes. We started talking and it turns out she was the voice of Elsa in Norway for Disney's *Frozen II*. She, along with other Elsas from around the world including Idina Menzel, would be performing at the Oscars.

"Will you sing a line?" I asked enthusiastically.

She obliged, belting out a tune that reverberated through the salon. I recorded it on my cell phone and later shared the impromptu video with our weekend show. She so sweetly shared the online post of our meeting to her followers around the time of my book launch.

When I meet anyone, I look for purpose, little clues, and surprises that might give me a hint as to why it might be a one-in-a-million encounter. I'm always asking: "Why are we really here?" I find the answer every day by doing something as simple as saying "Hello!" to strangers and letting the moment breathe.

I aim to speak and write the same way, talking to just *one* person who is watching and listening. We connect as writers and readers one-on-one. Some encounters in our life will only happen if we take time to stop, reflect, and communicate with people around us as if they are the headline. I'm constantly thinking: *What if I am meant to be a part of their story? What if they are meant to be part of mine?*

Adrienne Bankert is an ABC News National Correspondent and the author of *Your Hidden Superpower: The Kindness That Makes You Unbeatable at Work and Connects You with Anyone.*

Life of Pie

LYDIA FENET

When New York City came to a grinding halt in March 2020, my family was on a spring break trip in Colorado. My three kids, husband, and I arrived at the hotel only to find they had closed the entire mountain ten minutes earlier—the concierge was in tears as she delivered the news. I felt a rush of emotions come over me: disbelief, disappointment, and, ultimately, fear. I knew this was likely the beginning of a profound change to life as we knew it. But in my role as mom, I also knew that my reaction would set the tone for my family. "I have bad news and good news," I said to them, with a bright smile on my face. "The bad news is the mountain is closed. The good news is there is still tons to do."

Little did I know how wrong I was.

Almost overnight, every available activity in the ski village closed. Instead of waiting in lift lines, we waited for the hours to pass. Every day there were fewer and fewer people around until by day four we could walk around the entire ski village without seeing a single person. We moved into a house, which seemed preferable to staying in an empty hotel where my husband and I joked we felt like we were on the set of *The Shining*.

Our plans for feeding ourselves were completely upended, too. The choice to eat on the mountain or at restaurants in the nearby village disappeared, so we were left with an option that is totally normal for most people, but something you can easily avoid if you live in Manhattan: cooking.

My mom will tell you that I come by my lack of cooking skills honestly; my sister nicknamed her "Sally Crispy" because she couldn't seem to cook a meal without burning it or leaving the kitchen filled with smoke. After leaving home, I went straight from a college meal plan to a city where it was easy to find a million other things to do besides cook.

So when I found myself in snowy Colorado with nothing but time on my hands and nowhere to order takeout from, I thought: *Right. Time to figure this out.* But after a few days of experimenting with easier dishes, I threw in the towel and delegated the cooking to my husband. Luckily, he enjoyed it and, quite frankly, was much better at it. But, between supervising remote school for three kids two hours early on Mountain Time and trying to keep my team intact at work, I did find time to revisit the one thing in the kitchen that I loved doing: baking.

If we were good friends, you would know that my true motivation for baking is my love of tasting batter right before it goes in the oven (please don't lecture me on raw eggs; I've made it this far and I'm still standing). As the days in Colorado crept along at quite possibly the slowest pace humanly imaginable, I channeled my nervous energy into sweet recipes. At first, I revisited the easy stuff I used to make when I was little: cookies, banana bread, cakes, and a soon-to-be family favorite, pecan pie.

Growing up in Louisiana, there was a small pecan tree that grew in our backyard. During the spring months as the flowers grew, you could find me or one of my three siblings climbing the tree branches. As the sticky, hot days of summer receded, the pecans would grow and drop all over the ground below. That was our cue to get a bowl from the kitchen and gather as many as we could. Inevitably it became a competition—as everything was with my siblings.

When my mother had her fourth child, my grandparents' baby gift was a cook named Pauline whose job was to feed us a few times a week, giving my mom the freedom to focus on her newborn daughter and spend time with her other kids too. Pauline was supposed to stay a few months, but once my parents tasted her cooking, weeks turned into years.

While my parents loved her gumbo, fried okra, and crawfish étouffée, I was glued to her side for the desserts. Pauline made cookies and pies from scratch, rolling the dough out with a rolling pin, and then filling her pies with tart lemon meringue or molasses-thickened filling for pecan pie. I wasn't much help then, preferring to wait until she turned her back so I could stick my finger into the raw cookie dough or syrupy fillings before running out of the kitchen, but I will never forget watching her and how much my parents enjoyed eating her creations.

During the long days in Colorado when the snow was coming down too hard to go outside, I re-created memories of sitting in my childhood kitchen with my own kids, piling them on the counter so they could add ingredients, crack eggs, and mix the dough with their spoons. While I used pre-made pie crust instead of homemade, my kids never seemed to mind. When I turned around, I still pretended not to see them sticking their fingers in the filling when they thought I wasn't looking.

Many months later, we felt ready to return home. We arrived back into a changed New York in June. Gone was the bustling city we had left in early March. The streets were eerily quiet, and neighborhood spots were boarded up. As the weeks passed, we would run into a family on the street and shriek with happiness: "You are still here! Are you okay? How is everyone?" Although outside dining was reopening, we began to invite a few close friends over for dinner instead of venturing out.

My first pecan pie received raves, so I started making them any time we saw friends. I have probably made fifteen pecan pies since then—a few for my family, a few for dinners with another couple, and others for friends who were having a rough time. Sometimes it was a plain pecan pie, other times chocolate, sometimes with bourbon (if I was hoping to spice up the evening).

When I think back to our time in Colorado, I will remember the fear of the unknown as our country went into lockdown, but I will always be glad for the pause in our lives. It was a time to reconnect—both with myself and with my family. And it was a time to make new memories around a longtime childhood pleasure: baking a pecan pie.

🕒

Lydia Fenet is the author of the acclaimed book *The Most Powerful Woman in the Room Is You*. She is the Global Managing Director of Strategic Partnerships and Lead Benefit Auctioneer at Christie's Auction House, where she has worked for two decades. She has led auctions for more than six hundred organizations and raised over half a billion dollars for nonprofits globally. She is currently writing a follow-up book entitled *The Most Confident Woman in the Room Is You*.

What's in a Name? My Best Friends

MELISSA GOULD

I was on the phone with my guru recently and as we were hanging up, I said excitedly, "Oh, almost forgot to tell you: I got the gold hoop earrings I wanted! I found them online, on sale, *and* free shipping."

"Of course, you did," my guru responded. "It's because you're a manifestor, and when you're a manifestor, the universe provides."

A few days earlier, I had manifested a parking spot at Trader Joe's. I immediately called my guru to tell her that, too. She wasn't surprised then either. All she said was, "I love it!"

OK, so my guru isn't really a guru, but she does have a master's degree in spiritual psychology and she's also one of my best friends. I like to call her *my guru* because we go on long walks and ask for each other's opinions and we speak "universe" together. Her advice tends to come from her "loving" and when we are on our walk-and-talks, she will sometimes stop because she suddenly "feels called" to tell me something. Sometimes the "thing" is that my hair looks blonder or it's to ask me how I'm doing—*how I'm really doing*—and I tell her because we share our real lives with each other. Like when her mother was in hospice, I told her I'd light a candle. "I love you," she cried to me on the phone. I answered the way one of us always does, "I love you more."

I've always valued my close friendships, but there's something about having friends now, in my middle-aged years, that feels particularly meaningful. Our phones ping at all hours about everything best friends want to tell each other. Like the meals we've made or are thinking about making or have already eaten or are thinking about eating. We talk about our growing children, aging parents, our collective lack of sleep, and depleting hormones. We talk about the big and the small things that make up our lives simply because we want to share these things with people who get why we want to share them in the first place.

One of my other best friends and I once talked on the phone for twenty minutes with genuine curiosity and detail about why her Costco carries Nestlé chocolate chips and mine carries a generic brand. In fact, we *still* talk about it and may continue to talk about it forever, and that is why, out of all of my close friends, I think she could be my soul mate.

She and I met when we were in our twenties, we were there at each other's weddings and childbirths, and she, along with my sister, has forever been in the top three of my *in case of emergency* list. As a young*ish* widow, I take comfort in the fact that in my husband's absence, she has been the friend who is the most interested and vested in almost every decision I make. Decisions about my daughter (curfews, college, boys), my finances (sell, save, diversify), and whether or not I even needed the gold hoop earrings that my guru was so convinced I manifested. My soul mate was the one who drove me home from the hospital after my husband died, and I'm the one she first confided in twenty years ago when she fell in love with a woman—the woman who would later become her wife.

I share everything with my *soul mate–bestie,* and by everything, I mean *everything*. I've even been tempted to send her a nude photo of my new love, just so she can see, well, everything about him that I love.

Meanwhile, it's my *partner-bestie* who feels most like a sister (but my real sister is my sissy and she's my most *forever*-bestie). My partner-bestie and I fell in friend-love at first sight right there on our daughters' kindergarten playground. We even had a business together for a number of years, and although the business ended, our partnership did not. In fact, that is how we came to call each other "partner," although sometimes people think we are *partners* in a different way. Neither of us seems to mind.

My partner-bestie and I have literally traveled the world together, sharing a bed and a bathroom for extended periods of time, and we giggle like pre-teens with a mere glance or shrug in each other's direction. As a joke that only she would get, I once framed a photo of myself wearing a bikini and gave it to her as a gift. She laughed so hard, we both did—over seeing me on the beach, arms up, embracing life, my middle-aged jiggles exposed to the world—that we both cried and maybe even tinkled a bit.

When she got divorced and tiptoed into online dating, we both had to approve all viable candidates before she could even swipe right. We laugh about how our lives turned out, "The Widow and the Divorcée," she'll say.

"Who knew?" I'll respond. We shake our heads and sigh, not just over our losses, but also in gratitude that we not only *get* each other, but that we *have* each other.

What I cherish most about my girlfriends, even the ones without nicknames, is that my friends elevate me and give me license to *be* me. We see each other, in our complicated and simple messes, as mothers and wives and daughters and sisters and people in the world.

It's something that even my new love (who I affectionately refer to as *my beast*) commented on early in our relationship. "It's one of the things I love about you, baby," he said. "Your friends. The way you all relate to one another, it goes deep. Real deep."

Of course, I couldn't wait to share this news: *My beast gets me! He understands!*

I knew just who to call.

Melissa Gould is the author of *Widowish: A Memoir*. Her essays have been published in the *New York Times*, the *Los Angeles Times*, the *Washington Post*, *Buzzfeed*, and more.

A Gift by the Sea

NICOLA HARRISON

When my ex-husband, Manny, asked me to meet him for a drink on a biting December day in 2019, it seemed suspicious. We all got along well—my ex, our ten-year-old son, my new husband, Greg, me—and parenting apart was easier than it ever was when we were together. Still, I had the feeling I was about to get some momentous news. Trying to stay warm, I rubbed my hands together as I sat down across from him in the lounge at the Beekman Hotel just opposite the apartment Greg and I had recently renovated in downtown Manhattan.

"So," he said, taking a sip of his gin martini with a twist, the drink I'd never approved of because gin made him fiery. "I was thinking—we should all move to California."

I couldn't believe what I was hearing. We'd been married seven years, separated for two, and divorced for three. With his family and his job in Manhattan, moving to the West Coast had never been an option.

"I'm turning fifty next year; I hate my job, and I'm not in a relationship," he continued. "I'm ready for a change. So, if you guys are up for it, let's head West."

The truth is I'd always wanted to return to Southern California, where my parents lived and where I'd spent my teenage years, but our shared custody agreement cemented me in New York City indefinitely. To be exact, I had to live within a twenty-five-mile radius of the Empire State Building, according to the divorce decree. I loved

Manhattan and resigned myself to that arrangement, but I really missed my parents.

We lost my brother in a car accident when he was twenty-two and I was eighteen, and it made my parents and me cling to one another. In my final year of high school, after my dad went back to work, I'd drive home on my lunch break to check in on my mom to make sure she wasn't giving up. And yet after college, I still followed my dreams to New York City. I wanted to escape the grief and sadness that enveloped me. I wanted to start over.

I worked at a fashion magazine in Midtown. I got married and had a baby, and almost as soon as I did, I wanted to go back home. I didn't want some stranger watching my child a few days a week; I wanted my mom. After becoming a mother, I wrestled daily with the guilt I felt for leaving my parents, for not living closer, and for robbing my mom and dad of their chance to be the type of grandparents who lived down the street, or at least in the same town as their grandkids. Somehow I thought giving them a grandchild could help heal the pain of losing their child, but I hadn't bargained on how the distance would change everything.

The irony of my ex-husband's proposal was that three years prior, my now-husband, Greg, had uprooted his life in California and moved to New York. Also recently divorced, he'd been living in San Diego when we met, and, looking for a change of pace, he set his sights on Manhattan. Those first two years of our marriage were a whirlwind—in addition to buying and renovating an apartment, we had a baby. Greg was thriving as a dentist on the Upper East Side, and I published my first book and was working on my second. Life had been so busy, in fact, that we'd joked we'd be bored out of our minds in 2020. (I'll never make that joke again.)

* * *

"Let's do it," Greg said when I told him about Manny's sudden announcement.

"I thought you loved Manhattan," I said.

"I do, but I really hate the winters."

But it was more than that. Greg had taken one look at our baby Greyson and started missing his parents. I could relate. Ten years earlier, I'd felt the same way when Christopher was born.

So, a few weeks before the news of COVID-19 became a reality, before the city shut down and the schools closed, we put our freshly renovated apartment on the market. Miraculously, in mid-summer, while people were fleeing the city in hoards and the housing market was flooded with sales, we found a buyer.

In October we moved from Manhattan, New York, to Manhattan Beach, California, a block away from the ocean. We were smack in the middle between both sets of grandparents, forty-five minutes in each direction. Manny followed a month later and found a place a mile from us. We traded our boots and heavy down coats for flip-flops and shorts. After-school activities became boogie-boarding, jumping on the trampoline, and surf sessions.

But not everything was how I had pictured it. When we first arrived, my parents were watching the kids two days a week, their eyes smiling under their masks at being part of their everyday lives. But later, with COVID-19 cases in California soaring, my parents had to stay home. I was only able to write during the baby's naptime and after managing remote school. I think I saw Manny more than I did when we were married!

He had his fiftieth birthday just weeks after he arrived and, in the absence of his friends and family, we baked him a cake and threw him a party. In COVID times, this meant a barbecue on our patio with just the five of us: Greg, Manny, Christopher, Greyson, and me. Manny opened an expensive bottle of wine to celebrate.

"I've had this one for a while. Actually, I think it was one of our wedding gifts," he said casually as Greg handed him the decanter he'd salvaged in his divorce. The three of us said cheers and took a sip, and I couldn't help but laugh at how strange this all was. What a modern family we'd become in this post-divorce, mid-pandemic life!

One Saturday we all walked down to the beach together. As I watched Greg at the water's edge holding Greyson's hand while Manny and Christopher carried their surfboards into the waves, I thought: *This is not normal. Ex-spouses are not supposed to mingle with new spouses like this.* In New York, if Manny had stopped by most afternoons, I'd likely be stressing about boundaries and sticking to legal schedules. But here, I was grateful.

At some point I'm sure we'll get back to a routine. Christopher will start in-person school, and we'll return to our pre-COVID, pre-cross-country-move custody agreement of every other weekend and one night during the week. Both sets of grandparents will be able to see the kids without fearing for their lives, and I'll be able to get back to my writing schedule. But for now, I'm taking things one day at a time. When Greg and I lie in bed at night, the kids asleep and the house quiet, we listen to the sound of waves breaking on the beach and I feel at peace. We've been given a gift, I think to myself.

I just never imagined it would have been thanks to my ex-husband.

Nicola Harrison is the bestselling author of the novels *Montauk* and *The Show Girl*. Born in England, she is a graduate of UCLA and received her MFA from Stony Brook. She lives in Manhattan Beach, California, with her husband, two sons, and two high-maintenance Chihuahuas.

The Little Pink Unicorn

HEATHER LAND

The moment I became a mom was the moment I accidentally signed up to pee with the door open, to eat leftover chicken nuggets and soggy Cheez-Its for dinner, and to put each and every one of my own personal needs, wants, and desires on the back burner.

I'm not even sure how it happened. It wasn't a demand set forth by God or the universe. There was no ceremony or documentation signing my life away. It was just my self-sacrificing, devoted nature that spoke to my insides and told me that being a good mom meant that from now until the end of time, I would live only to serve the needs of my children. Having needs of my own was just, well . . . wrong.

What, small child? I have a cart full of groceries and have given away an hour and a half of my life to Walmart but you want to pitch a fit and go home?

Of course, darling. Let us be on our way.

And what's that? Mommy is right in the middle of talking to a friend, which I hardly do anymore, but you suddenly need my undivided attention?

Absolutely. Let me stop everything. I can finish this conversation when you graduate high school.

I sound bitter—allow me to clarify. I was raised by well-meaning people who showed me that the way to love was to be and do all things for all people all the time. My Christian upbringing and the almost-literal use of *John 15:13*—"Greater love hath no man than this, that a man lay down his life for his friends"—was proven to be the only way to live. I watched my father sacrifice every dream and desire he ever had to continually help a drug-addicted family member who never seemed to care quite as much as he did. I watched woman after woman let their own kids straight trash-talk them into submission as if this were the Godly way. I'm not here to judge. As a matter of fact, my first and natural tendency was to follow suit.

From the time my children were forming their eight-pound bodies in my belly, it was clear to me that my life was no longer my own, and surprisingly, I was thrilled! I could not wait to be a mom. But life around me didn't stop when my children exited my lower parts.

There was something else demanding my focus in my early years of motherhood: my failing marriage. Don't forget, I had dedicated myself to the very literal following of God's Word, which meant that my marriage could not, in fact, fail at all. There was no room in the scripture for context. Divorce was branded on my brain a mistake. I was even in ministry at the time, for goodness' sake!

I had to keep it together. Me. I. Never mind that it takes two to tango. In trying to be the best mother I could possibly be, I stayed in a toxic relationship that took my joy and my excitement for life. It took my energy and my happiness and my center.

There clearly needed to be a balance. But I didn't know the meaning of the word, until quite suddenly I did.

Enter counseling.

In my late thirties/early forties (better late than never), I realized that giving from a place of emptiness wasn't giving at all. I realized that if I truly loved the people I claimed to love, taking care of myself first was the best place to start. I knew that in order to be a whole human being and a good mother for my children, I had to leave my marriage. My children needed the real me, the best me, and this was the only way I could give it to them.

I won't keep you here much longer. And I won't go into detail. Just let me say this: If it wasn't for talking with my counselor and the little stuffed pink unicorn she made me purchase to represent my inner child, I don't know where I would be today. I know for a fact that I would be shedding way more tears, feel way more stressed, and be way more bitter and passive aggressive. I had no idea the amount of emotional weight I was carrying over past hurts from other people. And look, I'm perimenopausal—I can't afford to carry any more additional weight.

These days, I have a new perspective on self-sacrifice. I will always give my love, my time, and my attention to the ones I care about most. But from now on, that has to include me. I'll probably never quit tending to the needs of my children (even when they have their own), but I will continue to remember that I should love and tend to my own heart as well.

Case in point: I am currently writing three words at a time because my children are requesting various things as we speak and they aren't even little anymore. They're teenagers.

I know that this phase will end one day, and when it does I will cry a million tears and curl up in the fetal position for a solid month before inevitably enjoying the life of an empty-nester. I know that there will be many days ahead when I don't do it all just right—when I give too much, maybe even not enough. And when those days come, I will continue to reach for my little pink unicorn that lives beside my bed.

I will look at the little girl inside myself, calm her fears, and remind her that it's OK to cry. It's OK to hurt, to not be perfect. I will remind her to take a minute, each day, to care for herself so she can get back out there and live to love another day. And I will remind her that if and when her time comes, it's OK to talk to little stuffed unicorns.

Heather Land is a comedian and author of the books *A Perfect 10* and *I Ain't Doin' It.* Heather is living her best life in Nashville with her two precious children, Noah and Ava, and her new, extremely handsome husband, Stephen.

The Pursuit of Becoming

ABBY MASLIN

Two years ago, I found myself at a Barre3 studio pliéing to the beat of Rihanna alongside a group of ladies in commemoration of a friend's birthday. For an hour we stared into the mirror, gently pulsing our three-pound weights whilst assessing our form (donned, naturally, in stretchy yoga pants and matching tank tops that sported the catchy motto "*From barre to bar!*"). Afterward, we celebrated at brunch with too many Aperol spritzes.

It was a fun day, one I hadn't thought critically about until I read Jia Tolentino's essay "Athleisure, Barre and Kale: The Tyranny of the Ideal Woman," a stirring indictment of the superficial and exhausting quest for self-optimization widely adopted by a demographic of privileged white women like me.

In the past decade, I've grown accustomed to birthday celebrations involving vigorous exercise followed by vigorous drinking. This particular group of friends, a collection of fit, smart, and talented women in their thirties and forties, are an exhausting lot to keep up with. Many of us are educators in the public-school system, a job that suggests a certain degree of modesty or casual ambition, neither of which holds true in our case. Instead, we represent a growing demographic of high-achieving, multitasking female hustlers who have been conditioned to strive beyond our current state of evolution.

Among this group of women are multiple business owners, published authors, yoga instructors, design gurus, marathon runners, and mothers, with the majority checking off at least three of these boxes. In addition to all of that, we are also the founders of a now-defunct vegan lunch club, in which we once served elaborate multi-course meals in our classrooms during our twenty-minute lunch break, and a book club dedicated to diverse authors, anti-racist texts, and wine consumption. Not even a global pandemic has successfully been able to slow this group's compulsion for new hobbies and ventures.

Perhaps it's the culture of our city, Washington, DC, that demands a certain degree of perfectionism and Type-A orientation in order to assimilate. Perhaps it's Instagram, that insidious driver of comparison and discontent. But perhaps it's this particular season of life: the perplexing quest to find purpose after the mad rush to become educated, employed, and financially solvent has subsided.

In whatever case, friendships these days feel complicated, tinged with a whiff of competition. On occasion I remember myself at twenty-two, a chubby college graduate backpacking (well, mostly eating and drinking) my way through Australia with eight hundred dollars in my bank account, an amount I intended to stretch over five months. As I traveled the country coast to coast with my best friend, Claire, we convened over important decisions like, "Is it dangerous to sleep at a train station?" and, "How much money can we make picking zucchini?" We were not yet concerned with spin classes, salads, or the best brand of athleisure wear. Although we were undeniably privileged, with loving parents across the world willing to finance our return voyage, much of the joy of our friendship was predicated on our shared ability to problem-solve, to finagle a path to survival in the most absurd, untenable circumstances.

Reading Tolentino's piece, I felt far removed from the woman I'd once been and from that delicious sense of teamwork I'd experienced in past female friendships. If it's true that competition drives most everything in life, particularly the capitalistic hamster wheel described in the piece, I'm forced to contend that it may even drive relationships with friends. At times I've wondered (silently, of course) if anyone else in this well-intentioned circle is exhausted by the pursuit of becoming. To what purpose do our elaborate efforts serve? An internal void created by privilege? An underlying desire to stand out among a curiously impressive crowd? And what would it look like to work together, instead of simply alongside one another, in pursuit of a mission other than our individual self-optimization?

Women, I believe, are hyper-capable creatures. If left even remotely idle, some of us become magnetized to capitalistic candy: the newest fitness fads, mastering the Instant Pot, Chip and Joanna Gaines's latest line for Target, and even optical allyship with the trending social-justice causes.

These are particularly tempting directions to slip into, especially on the days in which the world feels too terrible or cumbersome to set right, and most especially on the days in which genuine self-reflection is tough. I love my friends. I enjoy many of our hobbies. (However, you will never again find me at a Solidcore class. Once was enough to make me question my sanity.) But I can't get around the idea that without constant intentionality and reorientation, I risk deferring to a caricature of myself, unable to get off this inexplicably consuming quest for idealism.

So, what does an adult woman really need from her female friends? Is it permission to deviate? To charter a new course? To quiet the call of capitalism, silence the patriarchy, and normalize rest (not as a reward for pain and suffering, but as its own sufficient entity)? What would it be like to just *be*—without the expectation of striving for more?

Women know well what it is to stand alongside each other: in the mirror at barre class, in the pixelated curation of our social media feeds, even at a protest. Perhaps what we need practice with is learning to work *with* one another: to identify and solve problems collaboratively, and to honor the success of the group, not simply the individual.

Thinking back to my post-college travels and the vast landscape of Western Australia, I can remember fumbling beside Claire, attempting to pitch a tent in the waning dusk. We howled at our own ineptitude, tossing wooden rods this way and that, hopelessly unable to construct anything that resembled a shelter. Unburdened by the need to appear skilled, we leaned into the moment's comic elements, conjuring gentleness and forgiveness, and a refusal to take one's self too seriously.

The pursuit of becoming demands we adopt a vigilant and critical lens toward ourselves, one that is too easily transferred to the people in our lives. But for a moment, in the desert, far away from a set of exacting standards and an impending era of rigorous idealism, that lens ceased to exist. As I laughed acceptingly at a work very much in progress, I felt remarkably complete.

Abby Maslin is the author of the *Washington Post* bestseller, *Love You Hard: A Memoir of Marriage, Brain Injury, and Reinventing Love*. She is also a public school educator in Washington, DC, where she lives with her husband, TC, and their two children. A nationally recognized speaker for traumatic brain injury and caregiving, Abby is an avid yogi and a devout coffee-drinker.

Snow and the Night Sky

JEANNE MCCULLOCH

The message was written in a spidery hand on a scrap of paper ripped from a legal pad, the edges ragged. It lay on the table in an unfamiliar kitchen, held down by a coffee mug. I had gone with my boyfriend, maybe he was already my fiancé, to visit his aunt in Weekapaug, Rhode Island. She lived alone in the family house and barely spoke a word to us, though from time to time we heard her moving along the hall upstairs, the uneven floorboards creaking in the dark house as the wind blew off the sea. We were just twenty-four.

"Your sister called to tell you Snow is dead." That was the message. I didn't see the lugubrious aunt again. I got on a train back to New York for the funeral of my childhood best friend.

Her real name wasn't Snow, it was Cathy. But Cathy didn't do justice to her flaxen blonde hair, it was too plain a name. We tried for a long time to come up with a counterpart for me, but my red-brown hair only conjured words like 'Rust" and "Irish setter"—for a while we tried "Terracotta," but it was too much of a mouthful.

Our mothers had met dropping us off at Sunday school in the local Episcopal Church, and bonded over the fact that both families had just arrived in New York from Europe, and we were beginning schools across the street from each other on the Upper East Side: Snow to the more conservative school, where, in 1968, girls wore Nixon buttons pinned in their hair ribbons; and me to the more progressive, where we wore black armbands and canvassed the Yorktown neighborhood for social-studies credit.

It's been said that you do not make friends, you recognize them. What did we recognize? A way of being easy with each other, I suppose. A love of the madcap. Shaky Super-8 movie footage shows us dashing around in my family's den wearing my mother's fur coats, the hems puddling at our feet.

When Snowflake the albino gorilla graced the cover of *National Geographic*, we spent entire Saturday afternoons in white turtlenecks and ballet tights, our hair tucked into my mother's white latex bathing caps, perched on the arms of club chairs and the backs of couches, munching imaginary bananas. We invented a language—it went *bwa, bwa, bwa*—that only albino gorillas could speak. On Sunday mornings, we zipped maroon choir robes over our neon-striped mini-dresses and fishnet tights and walked demurely up the aisle of the church, taking care not to let our chain belts clang against our hymnals.

During the spring we were twelve, Madison Avenue opened to pedestrian traffic on Monday evenings to encourage shopping, and families emerged from innocuous apartment buildings to congregate in the street. Mothers in sensible shoes walked the family dogs, some smoked cigarettes. Salesgirls from the cosmetics shop on 76th Street and the bakery on 73rd would stand on the curb offering free samples.

Snow and I would watch the sky as evening came on, making our pilgrimage to Baskin-Robbins on 84th Street. She was only allowed to stay out until nightfall, so as we walked we found names for the darkening sky. Faded denim, Robin's-egg blue, royal blue, brand-new denim, sapphire, indigo. At indigo, we'd turn around. "It's not technically dark yet," I'd say, "I still see some blue up there, there's still some light." So, we'd linger, eating our cones, then slowly turn down a side street and back to the corner of Lexington and 72nd Street to drop Snow off with her doorman.

We both had artistic dreams. We'd lay in bed on our weekend sleepovers and tell each other grand plans, our hands dancing in the air as we constructed futures for our lives. I was to be a writer, she was to be a painter, and she surely would have been a gifted one. She tossed it off lightly, but her talent was recognized early on. By the time she got to Yale she was named the Scholar of the House in the art department.

I remember at the time thinking of addiction as a big house. A house with loud music playing all the time, drowning out the sound of the phone ringing when those of us on the outside called. It was hectic in there, groups of damaged souls dancing and spinning into walls with chaotic euphoria.

Soon after we graduated from college, Snow slipped into that house quickly when I wasn't looking. Where the hell was I? Why wasn't I pounding on the door demanding she come out? I was on the outside somewhere, busy starting my own life, living in a tiny apartment on Horatio Street with a tall man and a magazine job that included petty cash.

In the last picture I have of Snow, she is standing with her dog Travis and a boy she met in art school. Her jeans are splattered with paint and rolled above her ankles, her blonde hair is matted, cut short in uneven chunks around her face as if she'd taken scissors to it in the dark. She had a column of rubber bands around her ankles, and more on her wrists, her car keys hung on a ribbon around her neck.

The image of that big chaotic house kept coming to mind at her funeral, and at the reception afterward in my family's living room. I saw myself standing outside that house, and I could not forgive myself for not looking up long enough to see her as she wafted by the window, as if that could lure her out. Even when I knew she was struggling, still I was standing outside with my hands in my pockets, staring down at the rough pavement, accepting the boundaries she'd put up.

The coroner reported pneumonia as the cause of death, and I imagine her body was so emaciated by then from heroin use that anything could have taken her out.

The train rumbled through the Connecticut countryside later that day as I returned to the tall fiancé in Rhode Island. Slowly the lights in the farmhouses along the route came on, the sky a faded denim blue. Still time to hang out, Snow would say, it's only technically dusk. Light lingers long in the New England summer sky. Gradually the clouds went from lavender to ash. Ten minutes later as we neared the New Haven station, the sky darkened to royal blue, then slowly to sapphire. Even so, there was an astonishing light that night; a profusion of stars promised clear weather ahead. There was no reason to leave yet, I was thinking, we can linger. There's so much left to do. But I was traveling through the New England indigo night alone.

The boys of our youth, now men in their sixties, still speak of Snow to me. The boy with the yellow socks, now a trial attorney in San Francisco. The boy with the madras jacket and the buck teeth, now a screenwriter in LA. The jazz musician. As they speak a light sparks and redirects, they're rummaging in their deep past for a glimpse of the golden girl none of them could catch, the pale goddess of their fevered adolescent imaginations. Always they ask: "Did you see it coming?"

Did I see it coming? After forty years, I still think of Snow when I look at the darkening sky. I've wondered what her art would be like, if our kids would know each other, if we'd teach them our monkey talk, and if she suddenly appeared, what we would say.

I do know one thing. I know we would recognize each other.

Jeanne McCulloch is the author of *All Happy Families: A Memoir*. She is a former managing editor of the *Paris Review*, a former senior editor of *Tin House* magazine, and the founding editorial director of Tin House Books. Her writing has appeared in the *New York Times*; *O, The Oprah Magazine*; *Vogue*; *Allure*; and the *North American Review*, among other publications. She lives with her family in New York.

Mission: Quiet the Stomachs

MALCOLM MITCHELL

It did not take a rocket scientist to tell we didn't have much money. It was most noticeable on the first day of school when other kids wore new shirts, crisp jeans, and fresh sneakers. But not having money wasn't so bad in the beginning, and neither was being hungry. We could sleep it off. We also learned drinking enough water from the faucet would briefly quiet the rumbling. If that didn't work, playing outside was a good distraction, but I never advised that. After you finished playing, the hunger came back with a vengeance, twisting, turning, and dropping its weight inside your stomach like a mad man waving fifty-pound dumbbells on a rollercoaster.

One morning, I stumbled into the kitchen and saw big Brother and baby Sister rambling through the cabinets, their stomachs just as mad as mine. Perhaps it was the *Nancy Drew* books, or desperation, that made me confident enough to devise a plan to quiet our stomachs. When the hunger took over our minds, when it grew too loud to be ignored, I went to the train tracks behind the house.

Weeds grew through the rails. You could witness a snake or two bathing in the middle of the tracks at certain times of the day. There were pockets of dirt where I could draw out my ideas like a pirate's treasure map. Once I had our plan drawn out, I called for Brother and Sister. I could always hear Brother before I saw him: "Didn't I tell you to stop yelling?" Then Brother would appear holding Sister's hand like he did at Grandma's funeral. If you followed the trail of tracks to the left, it spat you out behind the building where Ma went to pay bills. If you followed it to the right, you were thrown onto the main road in front of our cul-de-sac. On the other side of the road a convenience store sat bored and alone. There used to be a bread store right next to it, only a chain fence to separate the two. On our mission to quiet our stomachs, that convenience store was our mark.

DING DONG, the door played when Sister walked in. She moseyed to the left side of the store where she found Thunderhead the cashier. The bell did not break his focus from the summer-themed word search he was straining to complete. Facing the register, a gigantic scream escaped Sister's mouth, "*AAAAAAAAGGGGGGHHHHHHHH!!!!*" It reminded me of a wounded dog. Brother and I were twiddling our thumbs outside, peeking through the store window, awaiting the signal. We could hear Sister's wails through the glass.

Thunderhead's broken trance was our signal. In a panic, he made his way around to Sister. He disappeared behind the wall that separates the cashier from the rest of the store just long enough for Brother to creep in unannounced and dash behind a bushel of aisles. Sister's howls quieted the bell. Phase one, create a distraction: check.

Outside, I could see Thunderhead scampering to Sister's rescue, but her howls grew louder. As she filled the store with shrieks, Brother took a confidential stroll over to shopping aisle three. There, potato chips sat. Some hung high in the air. The best kind lay low, levitating right above the floor. Brother's moneyless hands cradled three bags and buried them in his oversized trousers. Who knew those black denim jeans from the Salvation Army would come in handy? He turned around to find the surplus of drinks in the gigantic refrigerators. After he concealed three cold drinks, orange for him, red for Sister, and purple for me, he moved towards the candy aisle. I requested a king sized bag of Skittles. Once the Skittles were lifted, Brother was scheduled to walk back toward the exit, hide behind the aisle closest to the door, and wait. Phase two, capture the food and drinks: check.

I figured after a few minutes of trying to placate Sister, Thunderhead would survey the store hoping to find Sister's parents. I was right. That was my cue. I did a couple jumping jacks to get my blood going, then sprinted inside. Once inside, I started panting, which was not part of the plan. My asthma had decided to join the mission. Out of all the things I could suck at, breathing just had to be one of them. The high-pitched squeaks that exited my mouth vanished after three deep breaths. As my lungs worked to catch up, both of my hands sat clumsily on my knees, my head free falling into my chest. I managed to get one sweaty finger in the air. "S... Sis... Sister..." Finally the words began to move. "Sister, I have been looking for you everywhere! What are you doing here? We gotta get home, now!" I marched over to her and thrust a sweaty palm onto her damaged sunset T-shirt. Her shirt tightened right before her neck followed my feet out the door.

DING DONG . . . As Thunderhead made his way back to the register, Brother burst out of the store and scaled the wall to his left until he got to the side of the building where he could not be seen. It felt like forever as we stood in the shadows of the tracks waiting for him, but we never left. Mom told us brothers and sisters always needed to be there for each other, no matter what. Thankfully, sixty seconds was enough time for Brother to be able to coast from the side of the store unsuspiciously, cruise across the street, and find us waiting.

Phase three, the exit: check.

We walked further down the tracks until we found a small strip of rail, a spot that could fit the three of us side by side. Brother pulled the chips out of his pants; one bag managed to slide all the way down. He had to take off his right sneaker to get it out. He pulled the orange soda out of his front left pocket, red soda out of his front right pocket, and my grape soda out of his back pocket. He stashed the Skittles in his socks. We sat in silence, with only the sounds of chips being shoved in our mouths to keep us company.

I knew what we did was not right. I wondered if Brother and Sister felt the same. I wondered what Ma would have said if she found out. I wondered if other kids had to do stuff like that to feel full, too. It was wrong, but as I ate the chips, my stomach quieted and my mind followed.

🕒

Malcolm Mitchell was drafted by the New England Patriots in 2015 and became a Super Bowl Champion in February 2017. Among Malcolm's numerous awards and accomplishments both on and off the field, he considers discovering a love of reading his greatest achievement. Malcolm has authored and published children's books, including *My Very Favorite Book in the Whole Wide World*, created a youth literacy initiative called Read with Malcolm, and established Share the Magic Foundation to transform lives through literacy.

Let's Just Meet Here Every Day

LINDSAY POWERS

A couple months before COVID-19 swept the world, a new playground opened a couple doors down from where we lived in Brooklyn. It was usually packed with kids playing while parents huddled around chatting or zoning out on their phones—a brief respite from the all-consuming work of raising little people.

The playground was our fallback when our four-year-old and six-year-old were climbing the walls. Unlike suburban playgrounds, which are usually empty because everyone has giant backyards and finished basements, city playgrounds are vibrant and full: a real slice of life. You never know who you'll meet, but you do know you'll never be alone. Kids organically start playing together, and before you know it you're hanging out with another adult and everyone feels a little less lonely.

In the COVID New York City spring, the streets were eerily empty and quiet, punctuated only by endless sirens. Schools and restaurants were shuttered. Jobs were lost or remote. Every day brought news of another friend infected, a mentee who died, a colleague who faced "long hauler" symptoms. A padlock was put around the gate of our beloved playground, and, for the first time since it opened, it was silent.

That's when we knew we had to get out of the city.

We rented an Airbnb for a month in rural Massachusetts, and then, after a couple calmer days there (no ambulance noises! a giant yard!), we panic-booked a farmhouse in upstate New York for another month. We hunkered down. Instead of visiting local playgrounds, we kicked around a ball in the backyard. We could count on one hand the number of people we exchanged words with.

When we returned to Brooklyn in August, nothing was the same, but the playground was open and people were there. As I watched my kids joyously run around and play with others, I felt relief wash over me. A few days later, we met up there with a close friend whose son was born days after my second son. While we were gone, she'd given birth to another baby, a daughter. "Let's just meet here every day at 4 p.m., OK?" she said. I agreed.

To other parents, I said the same: "Let's just meet here every day at 4 p.m., OK?"

Soon, we had a motley crew of neighborhood families meeting every day around 4 p.m., rain or shine, snow or heat. Our kids ranged from two months old to seven years old. The only thing many of us had in common was that we lived within a walkable distance to this playground, and we all felt traumatized by COVID. As a result, we had a silent language: Masks were non-negotiable. We brought extras in case our kids' got wet or lost, which happened not infrequently. Adults socially distanced, and we kept the kids distanced as much as possible. My husband and I joked that the playground was our entire social network, and many times, it was the only time we went outside all day.

We found our "pod" there. There was a mom who had been laid off from her job in marketing, so now was homeschooling her two young daughters; the energetic babysitter who was always down to be "it" at tag and who handed out homemade granola bars. A former first-grade teacher who moved to New York City months before the city shut down regaled us with stories about her small Florida hometown and their denial of the virus that left us feeling so scarred.

* * *

There was the dad who lost his job when the restaurant where he worked locked down and the couple who were both artists, the wife figuring out her next career move while taking computer programming classes and wrangling remote kindergarten. There was the lawyer dad who started taking all his conference calls from a park bench. There was the mom who was on the cusp of launching her personal-chef business, her husband anxious about his job security as international borders closed—both now buried in caring for their two children with myriad special needs.

We had nothing and everything in common. Financial fears. Fears over whether we'd get sick or whether we'd already had COVID-19. Fears over careers paused or temporarily derailed. But still the conversation flowed. Recipes were exchanged. An impromptu book club was formed when a handful of us decided on the spot we'd read *The Vanishing Half.*

Our kids invented games, including one called "praying mantis" that involved chasing each other to a base. Both my children learned how to ride two-wheel bikes. Another kid perfected his football spiral. They all learned how to climb the monkey bars.

As the pandemic dragged on, holidays were celebrated at the playground. On Halloween, the parents spread out so our costumed kids could trick-or-treat among us. We made sure we had a variety of treats so that the child with a super-rare genetic disorder and special diet felt included. "This is more fun than normal Halloween!" more than one parent said, as we handed out mini pumpkins and stickers for the kids to decorate.

The day after Thanksgiving, we gathered for a Black Friday play date. On New Year's Eve, we planned a piñata smashing in the basketball court so we could give 2020 the sendoff it deserved.

* * *

Not every day was perfect. The kids fought when the ball wasn't kicked to them enough, or they'd had a rough day at school. One kid became a bully, which we tried to gently remind ourselves could be a reaction to the uncertainty his parents faced after both losing their jobs. Some days I would announce to the other parents, "I am in a serious funk!" and drop the pretense of small talk. Sometimes they would do the same. We were all not ourselves, we agreed.

But in other ways, we were more ourselves than before. It was freeing to be able to shrug my shoulders and say "eh" when people asked how I was doing, instead of presenting relentless happiness and drive. It was reassuring to hear that everyone felt anxious and unsure about the present and what was next. Somehow, in our shared uncertainty and bewilderment, we found comfort.

I didn't know when we'd go back to some semblance of "normal." I didn't know when schools would close, or open, or when vaccines would arrive. But I knew if my family came to the park at 4 p.m., there would be somebody for my kids to play with, and somebody—a lifeline—for us to reach out to from six feet apart.

Lindsay Powers is the author of *You Can't F*ck Up Your Kids*, and a digital content consultant whose writing has appeared in the *New York Times*, the *Washington Post*, *New York* magazine, and many other nationwide outlets.

I'm Here for You

REV. LYDIA SOHN

I've been a bridesmaid seven times. I've hosted even more baby showers. Whenever you're going through a tough time, I'll call in sick at work and meet with you over many cups of coffee (or wine, whichever you prefer), with lots of nodding, *mm-hmm*ing, and thoughtful questions to help you get to the root of why you're upset and what you need to do next.

What I'm trying to say is: I'm a good friend. I even help others to be the same. For instance, I remind my husband of his friends' birthdays so he can send them thoughtful texts or emails.

And while I admit that some of my good-friend-nature derives from a need to be liked, most of it truly does come from a genuine and authentic place. I'm a deeply relational person who likes being around others and connecting with them in meaningful ways. So, it makes sense that I'm also a minister whose full-time job consists of connecting with and caring for others.

But then something happened that severely limited my ability to be a good friend. That something has two parts, each one intensifying the other. First, I had two children. Second, the arrival of my more recent child coincided with the COVID-19 pandemic.

A particularly vexing thought continuously reverberates through my mind during this pandemic: *I can't believe there were ever moments in my life when I thought I was busy*. I scoff at single, pre-pandemic Lydia. *You could have written like four books with all that free time!*

Looking back, I realize I spent that free time doing what I loved most: sleeping, reading, and being a good friend—all of which has been taken away from me to an alarming degree.

* * *

But it's my lack of ability to do that last thing that pains me the most. Especially because, if there ever was a time people needed good friends, it's right now.

At present, four of my closest friends are on the brink of divorce. Most of them have already separated their belongings from their spouse's and moved out. Other friends are battling depression from prolonged isolation and lack of support. One lost her mom to COVID-19.

On the rare chances I'm available to chat on the phone with one of these friends, my heart aches for them—and for me. I feel powerless and wish I could do more, so much more. I want to get on a plane and hold them while they break down and sob. I want to cook meals for them because I know they forget to feed themselves. I want to play with their kids and help them with their homework so my friends can keep their jobs.

When I have a moment to sit down and carefully consider actually doing any of this, I'm confronted with all of the obvious practicalities and downstream implications: Who would entertain and feed my own children? How would I pay my bills if I stopped working to be there for my friend? What if I contract the virus on my travels to or from my friend's house?

My four-year-old son yelling from the bathroom to help him wipe his butt snaps me out of my brainstorming in an instant.

As any parent knows, time poverty didn't start with COVID-19. But the pandemic has greatly exacerbated an already all-too-obvious reality for parents: Children are our greatest and most vital gifts, but they are also the most effective time-sucks God ever created. With additional restrictions on work, shopping, day care, schooling, where we can go, and what we can do, the impact of COVID-19 has significantly narrowed our options for time dedicated to ourselves and those we care about most deeply.

So, who do we turn to when we are falling apart, especially us parents of young children? Perhaps most obviously, some of my friends, including myself, have the good fortune of family support. But nobody can deny the unique gifts that good friends offer during distressing times.

Many of us don't feel as judged by our friends as we do our parents. We dish out more raw versions of our marital conflicts because if we conveyed the same version to our mothers, could she accept our spouses in the same way? As the great spiritual writer Anne Lamott wrote in *Almost Everything*, "To have a few amazing friends on this side of eternity, this sometimes grotesque amusement park, is the greatest joy . . . We cannot depend solely on spouses to dump on, to share our intimate thoughts with or reveal our deepest truths to. Trust me, they have been through enough just living with us."

Online therapy has skyrocketed during the pandemic, but once again highlighting the particular benefits of friendships, therapists can't help pack boxes or deliver meals made with love.

Though, I've noticed one thing during this phase of my life when I have very little time; a magical observation that defies the laws of physics. This observation feels like a secret because of how little it's mentioned. Or it's drowned out by the incessant and cacophonous "I don't have enough time for . . . " chorus.

That secret is this: Abundance is tucked within scarcity.

Like the butterfly hidden within the chrysalis, eventually eclipsing its original state, we can access this abundance by releasing our constant refrain that "we never have enough—."

It's not a lie. Pandemic-mommy-Lydia has less time to herself. Time for pre-children Lydia was like an ever-flowing river that I could drink from whenever I pleased, compared to what it is now: a puddle in a parking lot—paltry, scattered, and always mixed with a thousand other undesirable substances.

What's interesting, though, is that now I treat time with so much more care and intention. The rare moments I'm able to steal away for myself are infinitely more valuable. What used to take me a week to accomplish, I can now complete within two hours. The reverse also holds true. I used to spend entire weekends binge-watching Netflix only to feel a fraction of the restoration I feel from what I do now to refresh myself: an hour of getting lost in my most recent book from the library and a half-hour power nap.

It works the same way with my friendships. I can't hop on a plane to spend a weekend with my best friend or even have several hour-long phone conversations like we used to. But she's always on my mind as I change my baby's diaper, cook dinner, go on a walk. And, occasionally, I'll receive a stroke of insight in regards to her divorce, a thought I know will soothe her aching heart. "I realized on my walk today," I say, "that he did you a favor. He would've kept making you feel insufficient. I don't want to rush you through this dark tunnel of grief, but I promise you that, with time, you'll emerge on the other side of this a more powerful and authentic version of yourself."

Where once my words were plentiful but trite, now they are sparse but substantive. They hold a truth and gravity that can only come from a friend who loves her deeply and thinks about her day in and day out.

"And," I continue, "even though I can't physically be there for you in the way I want to be or used to be, you know I'm always here for you."

"I know," she says. She's telling the truth and so am I.

Rev. Lydia Sohn is a Southern California–based writer and minister. During the pandemic, she made a life-altering decision to leave her full-time job at a church to become a minister to the public through her website, and raise her two young kids with more flexibility. She is one of the four inaugural Moms Don't Have Time To Fellows.

MOMS
DON'T HAVE
TIME TO
WRITE

Can a Writer Be Too Emotional? Asking for a Friend

AIMEE AGRESTI

I had seen this trick before: numbers on my phone shape-shifted as I tossed and turned. First 1 a.m., then 2 a.m., then 3. My research suggested insomnia: It had been going on for weeks and the heroine in my upcoming novel was an insomniac.

Was it nervous energy? Things had definitely amped up as I got closer to the Zoom launch of my fifth novel. Or perhaps my body was involuntarily conscripting me into a method-acting exercise. Was I becoming my character? Because *that* would be completely ridiculous. Although, now that I thought about it, my body did have a history of going a little haywire around my writing life.

The first time my Writer Self hijacked my Otherwise Rational Self was a million years ago (or fifteen-ish). I had spent months sending out a still-in-progress collection of interwoven short stories to agents, to no avail. Until finally one evening I received a miraculous email from the hero who would become my agent: She liked my writing but story collections from unknown writers were a no-go. But there was a catch: Since my intertwined stories actually read like a novel, if I revised it she would represent me. *Yes!*

I went to sleep elated: *I have an agent! I'm writing a novel!*

The next morning I awoke, still buzzing, as I headed to my boyfriend's apartment with balloons and a gift bag: It was his birthday. I planned to surprise him and pick up his favorite breakfast on the way.

But somehow in those few blocks of DC's Dupont Circle, my excitement curdled to fear. The buzz had bloomed into full-blown panic by the time I reached the coffee shop. My internal voice was screaming: *Obviously I was only writing stories because I was scared of writing a novel. Could I figure it out fast enough to hold this agent's interest?* Sweaty and lightheaded with a dash of nausea, I placed my order for an egg-and-cheese and then promptly blacked out.

When my eyes flickered open, faces huddled above me. Why were they *staring* at me? Why did one look like the Edge from U2 with the goatee and the beanie? Where *was* I? Was I hallucinating?! How much U2 had I been listening to?! The faces receded and a ceiling came into focus. No hallucination: I was actually lying on the coffee shop's freakishly hard floor. I would later discover a giant bruise on my thigh, a memento.

The-Edge-But-Not-the-Edge helped me to my feet, someone gathered my balloons and gift bag, and everyone caught me up like *I* was a show I had missed. I had collapsed! *Twice!* The shop owner had just begun grilling me about my medical history when sirens whooped and an ambulance arrived, shattering all hope of a quiet exit.

At the hospital they ran a bunch of tests, hooked me up to a glucose drip, and determined that I was dehydrated and, sure, maybe stressed out (not a medical term). I also learned an important lesson: If you show up in the ER with a bunch of balloons, everyone wants to help because you seem like a lot of fun.

But I unfortunately didn't learn much else. Two published novels later, I managed an even more absurd sequel to this episode.

This time I was nine months pregnant with our second son (reader: I married the birthday-balloon boyfriend) and my then-publisher had just dropped the option on the third tome in my young-adult trilogy. It was a numbers game, I understood: I just hadn't sold enough of the first two books. I remained totally calm on the phone, then pushed past the crush of failure to greet the babysitter, kiss my three-year-old goodbye, and duck out to Back to School Night.

En route to the metro, still replaying the conversation, spiraling in fear that my fiction career was imploding, I started to feel . . . funny. *Contractions*-funny. *I-might-have-a-baby-so-I-better-not-get-on-the-train* funny. I summoned my husband from an event honoring a senator he had worked for and we went to the hospital, where we spent three hours watching ABC's Thursday night lineup until my contractions stopped. Basically it was a date night. My doctor prescribed me a glass of wine. (I didn't follow his orders, but made a concerted effort to chill.)

The book came out the following year in German (*danke* to my wonderful German publisher) and in English years later. The baby came out—just in English—a week after the false alarm. He was perfect; I was lucky.

My Otherwise Rational Self, my cool Jekyll, knows this is no way to behave. Enough with these physical manifestations of writing-life anxiety! But my Writing Self is a drama-queen Hyde, branding these hijinks as *passion*. She argues maybe extreme emotional responses are warranted if you were, say, the daughter of a librarian and grew up harboring secret novel-writing dreams. Or *maybe* you wrote fiction for years in the off-hours through other jobs. And *maybe* the fear of blowing this amazing chance to keep writing fiction short-circuits your system occasionally.

Maybe, at the very least even your Rational Jekyll could accept that it's *passion* keeping you up till 4 a.m. And maybe the whole emotional mess that is YOU-writing-a-novel will happen again on the next book and maybe that's OK.

Maybe next time, your Jekyll will finally lean into its Hyde and call this zaniness what it truly is: your process.

Aimee Agresti is a journalist and author of the novels *Campaign Widows, The Summer Set,* and *The Gilded Wings Trilogy*. She lives in the Washington, DC area with her family.

Beneath the Surface

ESTHER AMINI

My father, in his thunderous baritone voice, always made it clear that books were noxious, toxic—the enemy. I grew up a first-generation American in a Jewish-Iranian home that tenaciously held onto the values and beliefs of Mashhad, Iran's most fanatically religious city.

My parents came from a place that kept girls out of school and far from the written word. The prevailing wisdom at the time was that female illiteracy was a God-given gift. The inability to read and write is what shaped young girls into supreme wives. Even though I was born in New York City and grew up in Kew Gardens, Queens, this was the ancient ethos my father hauled from Iran into our home. Despite his preaching, I secretly pined, in a hushed minor key, for college.

Beginning with first grade, I forged Pop's signature on every report card—not because I did poorly, but because I did exceptionally well. It wasn't until I reached high school that my father demanded to see my grades. My stomach cramped as he slowly read out loud each subject with its shimmering *A*. Pop's veined eyes bulged as he cursed the day he stepped foot in America. It was as if he had discovered I was a drug addict, mainlining heroin, and all of my *A*s were discarded needles. With a reddening face, while pulling at his thick white hair, he swore that his one and only daughter would never reach her desired destination: America's brothel—college.

I didn't grow up with visions of becoming a fiery and fierce Katharine Hepburn, nor did I have dreams of matrimony and motherhood. All I knew was that I loved to read. But I lived in fear as I secretly read books, plays, poems—whatever contraband I could stealthily smuggle into my bedroom. Under the covers, in a cold sweat, with flashlight in hand, I thumbed through *The Life of Houdini* while terrified of being caught.

"In Iran we suffered anti-Semitism," Pop admonished. "We escaped and immigrated to America, to live freely and openly as Jews—not as Americans. Not to end up cursed with a daughter who wants school." But I remained unswayed. Chasing what I wanted, I secretly sent out college applications and continued to forge Pop's signature; my rendition had only improved with time.

When I announced I was moving into Barnard College's all-female dormitory, Pop decided to end his life. He stopped eating, stopped working, and no longer shaved. I was terrified by my father's rage and his ten-day suicidal hunger strike. But battling my inner critic accusing me of patricide, I moved into the dorms anyway. On that mind-scrambling day, I summoned Mom's strength, drew from her ore, extracted her obstinance, accessed her inner outlaw, and made myself more similar than dissimilar.

To my deep relief, my father didn't die when I left. But still afraid of losing him, I came home every Friday and stayed through Saturday, hoping to show Pop that living in a dorm had done no damage, college hadn't made a dent: I hadn't learned a thing, I was unchanged—still his. How could I admit I was reading Betty Friedan's *The Feminine Mystique* and spending days at the Metropolitan Museum of Art studying Medieval Christian frescoes?

Having jumped insurmountable hurdles, I had achieved my one and only wish—to be educated. I was the first female from my matrilineal and patrilineal lines to attend grade school and become literate. After graduating from Barnard, I was certain I would never need to scale another mountain. For me, Kilimanjaro was college—climbed and conquered. Pocketing my B.A. in Art History, I returned to my family's Persian carpet business and worked as their secretary.

It was only years later, when my peers were plateauing, that I found myself gearing up again. A surge of energy had been quietly building its own momentum. By now, my aging father had mellowed. Preferring silence over speech, he turned inward, keeping to himself, no longer in a Cold War with the outside world. The voice of Mashhad with its prohibitions and limitations, which he fervently lived by, became an occasional murmur.

As if rushed by tidal waves, I returned to school, became a psychoanalytic psychotherapist, married an American, birthed a son and a daughter, and picked up a paint brush. I dove into pigment, painting furiously, making up for lost time. Mixing fleshy heaps of color, I'd scoop, fling, and scrape, painting shapes and forms that emerged from some unknown place. Alizarin crimson, burnt umber, Indian yellow, and phthalo blue became another language.

And at the same time, I was building a private practice, working with patients, teaching, and supervising therapists. Then in my sixties, I decided to write. Autobiographical short stories were rolling out of me fast and furious. To my shock and delight, they were warmly received. Another gust of energy propelled me into writing a memoir. It was about my parents leading a hidden life in the Iranian city of Mashhad, pretending to be other than who they were in order to survive, and how later I grew up in New York City doing the very same—hiding books, concealing myself, and living underground.

Looking back at those Ivy League days, I had no clue as to what lay within, what I would feel compelled to do, and where it would take me. I just feared my burning drive to attend Barnard College would turn me into my father's assassin. Once I knew Pop had survived, I felt flashing sparks stir and flicker.

So much laid dormant, buried beneath the surface, patiently waiting to bud.

Esther Amini is an artist, psychotherapist, and author of the debut memoir *Concealed: Memoir of a Jewish Iranian Daughter Caught Between the Chador and America.*

Camera Broken, Vision Renewed

TERRI CHENEY

Back when I was a practicing attorney and still had plenty of money to burn, a friend asked me to go on safari to Africa with her. I remember the evening well—I'd had a relapse of my bipolar disorder only a few weeks earlier, and had just come out of a mental hospital following a suicide attempt where they'd medicated me until I was sky high. We were at a sushi bar, it was extremely noisy, and I had to ask her to repeat herself. It took longer for her to ask the question than for me to answer yes. I was manic, I knew it, and I didn't care.

Africa sounded glorious, the solution to all the problems that had driven me to overdose. I had thought, like a fool or a child, that life was inherently fair, that all one needed to be happy was to work hard and reap the rewards. Well, I'd worked very hard—being an entertainment attorney was extremely stressful. And I suppose I'd been rewarded, at least in tangible terms. But I wasn't happy. Life hadn't turned out as I'd expected—money and prestige didn't cure my depression; they weren't the panaceas I'd been brought up to believe they would be. I needed a desperate change of scenery as far away from the law as I could get, and the wilderness of Africa promised exactly that.

It didn't take me long to book the most sumptuous trip I could arrange—the best safari package available, planned to the very last minute with wonders. My father, always my confederate in manic enterprises, bought me a super-deluxe Nikon camera to record my trip. It cost way more than even I'd have been willing to pay, but I think he fancied the idea of saying, "My daughter? Oh, she's off on safari right now." He stoked my dreams, as he always had, and, by the time I left for Nairobi, I was so excited I didn't sleep for the entire twenty-one-hour flight.

We spent a few days in the city and then the real trip began: three weeks on the Masai Mara, the vast expanse of plain populated by the indigenous Masai tribe and hordes of wild animals. The safari guide promised we'd see our fill of lions, elephants, crocodiles, giraffes, zebras, leopards, cheetahs, etc. It all sounded marvelous, although I doubt he knew how empty I was, and how much it would take to fill me.

But then, on the very first day of our trek, we spotted a pride of lions. They were more beautiful than I'd ever imagined they could be—tawny gold and sinewy, stretched out in the blazing sun under an acacia tree. There were five of us in the jeep, and we let out a collective sigh of satisfaction: It was *National Geographic* perfect. The guide maneuvered the jeep so we could take pictures, and just as he got us into close range, the male lion lazily mounted one of the females. I started clicking away, too eager to wait until we stopped moving. Right at that moment, the jeep hit a bump and the camera went flying out of my hands, landing with a distinct thud only yards away from the rutting male.

"No!" I screamed, and the lion looked over. The safari guide put his hand over my mouth and forced me back down in my seat.

That night, after the lions had left, one of the Masai camp attendants recovered my camera and brought it to me. As I'd feared, the lens was shattered. All I could see when I looked through it was darkness—pitch-black darkness, the color of dashed hopes and dreams. Being surrounded by so much visual splendor with no way to record it for posterity seemed to me to be the cruelest of punishments.

Africa was supposed to rescue me, but instead it was turning out to be just another illusion of happiness.

I went to bed feeling frustrated with the universe and furious with myself for not having bought travel insurance. Short of giving up and going home, there was nothing I could do to remedy the situation. Money was of no use to me this far from civilization; there was nowhere to buy a new camera or get this one fixed. I finally fell asleep, cursing God, Nikon, and most of all, my dreams.

Since life wasn't conforming to my exquisitely planned agenda, I was forced to set my expectations aside. At first, I tried taking notes on what I was seeing so I would remember it all. But Africa proved too big for that; its marvels were too many and too much for my pen. I gave up after a few days of frantic scribbling in the adventure journal I'd bought for the trip. Words couldn't begin to capture the brilliant colors of the savanna, or the immense empty sweep of the sky. My attempts to sketch what I was seeing were also hopelessly inadequate, a mockery of the magnificence surrounding me. In the end, I simply had to open my eyes and my heart and hope that I could cram enough into my memory to sustain me when I got home.

It was a turning point—not just in my trip, but in my life. I was thrust into the present, in all its unmitigated glory and occasional discomfort. Over the next three weeks, I encountered a starving Masai village, not from the neat distance of a viewfinder but right up close, with flies swarming in my eyes and my nose. I watched a flock of flamingos blot out the sun and turn the entire sky pink. I felt the thunder of elephants, heard the vicious snap of a crocodile's jaw on its prey. I nuzzled noses with a giraffe. Without the distraction of chronicling my experiences, I had no choice but to take them all in as they happened, and let them overwhelm me.

I realized then how limited my life had become: how carefully planned and utterly devoid of serendipity. What room was there for wondrous discovery, when everything had already been figured out? In the next few decades I'd likely go from associate to partner, from single to married, from young to middle-aged to old. From the openness of the African vista, my life looked like a death sentence to me.

The irony of this—and of so much else—didn't escape me. Only a few months before, I had tried to kill myself; but now, I truly wanted to live—*really* live, not just exist according to a smothering schedule. The world had laid itself bare before me, and all its opportunities were mine for the taking. If a little Masai girl could sing and dance despite her deprivations, what right had I to be depressed? Where, in all my wealth and abundance, had I misplaced gratitude?

So when I got home, the first thing I did was quit my job. I had no idea what would come next, and I liked it that way. I found a less stressful, less prestigious law firm where I could work part-time from home, an unheard-of thing in those days. And I started to write. Like everyone else, I knew I had a book in me that I'd never had time to open. I missed the money, but little else.

I was on a new safari—my second great adventure of a lifetime.

Terri Cheney is the *New York Times* bestselling author of *Manic: A Memoir* and *Modern Madness: An Owner's Manual*. Her life story was portrayed by Anne Hathaway in the Amazon Prime Video series, *Modern Love*. She now devotes her advocacy skills to destigmatizing mental illness.

In the Time of Corduroys

JEANINE CUMMINS

I grew up in the time of corduroys and mustard-yellow kitchen appliances. We had bad haircuts and built our own treehouses with hammers and scavenged wood. Our bicycles had swoopy handlebars, and we rode them far from home without supervision. When we played flag football, the assembled teams did not account for gender, size, or skill. Our teams, like our suburban DC neighborhood, were diverse and integrated: Black, Jewish, Korean, Puerto Rican, white, Ecuadorian, Japanese, Indian.

The language of self-identity did not exist then, but that didn't prevent us from noticing one another. Our families cooked different foods at home, but in large part, we all had Doritos in our Strawberry Shortcake lunch boxes. I thought my friend Debbie was the most glamorous girl in the first grade because the stacks of colored beads on the ends of her braids clacked against each other when we hung upside down from the jungle gym. We hatched a plan for her to put beads in my hair, too. She brought a comb, some tinfoil, and a stash of beads to my house after school. It did not turn out like we hoped.

Like many on our street, mine was a family of mixed heritage and ethnicity: We were Irish and Puerto Rican. There was other stuff in there, too, but the Irish and Puerto Rican roots were the ones that presented themselves in my life in meaningful ways. When I was little, we spoke Spanish at home. And my dad liked to say that even before I spoke English, I could sing Clancy Brothers' songs with a credible Irish accent. I was proud of these details because they were the features of my origin story, the way I positioned myself in the world. This is who I was: a Spanish-speaking, Irish-singing kid who desperately wanted beads that would clack whenever I shook my head. I was a super–Catholic Navy brat, the deacon's kid. I was bad at T-ball, but good at Double Dutch. These were the things that mattered.

But as I got older, I was unprepared for the rigid segregation of the real world. When I started driving, I noticed how often I got pulled over when I had Black friends in the car. At college in Baltimore, the student dining halls were almost entirely self-segregated; I didn't know where to sit. I was decidedly uncomfortable in the almost all-white room, literally separated from our fellow students (of color) by a glass wall. Neither was I brave enough, at first, to venture into that other room without an explicit invitation. I didn't feel entirely comfortable in either space.

This was years before I encountered the rapidly evolving vocabulary of self-identity, a language I still don't speak fluently. (I think only millennials are native speakers). But I've spent the intervening years grappling, sometimes clumsily, with the question of my identity and how to articulate it. My grandmother, Maria de los Angeles Quixano, was born and raised in San Juan, where my father spent part of his childhood. He attended elementary school in Santurce and flew his kite on the soaring green at El Morro. In his life, I'm quite certain my father never uttered the phrase "I identify as," but he considered himself white, as did his proud Puerto Rican mother. Incidentally, a St. Louis country club disagreed with her self-assessment; when Maria became a member, they refused her access to the women's locker room, assigning her a locker in the staff room instead. In their appraisal, she wasn't white enough.

I don't remember when I personally began using the word "Latino," but it didn't appear on the U.S. Census form until the year 2000, when I proudly checked the box. On the same form, I also checked "white," because even as the language of identity emerged and expanded, being Latino was never a racial designation. For me, those two ways of identifying have never been separate; I am white and Latina, both, together, not hyphenated. My family has always been evidence of this truth: Latinos come in different colors.

In recent years, I've felt a tightening calcification in conversations around identity, a pressure (both internal and external) to define precisely who I am, using just a narrow handful of words. I never considered that this might be problematic until 2020 when, for reasons too complicated to enumerate here (but loosely having to do with the fact that I wrote a novel in which most of the characters are Mexican and Central American), my race and ethnicity came under intense public scrutiny. My identity was adjudicated most furiously by the denizens of Twitter, where I was quoted recognizing myself as white, as if acknowledging the privilege conferred by my whiteness somehow erased the equal fact of my being Puerto Rican. As if I couldn't be both, so I'd chosen whiteness, thereby abdicating access to my identity as a Latino person. My now-broken Spanish was publicly ridiculed, and at the ugliest moment, there was even a suggestion that I'd dyed my dark hair and gotten a fake tan, altering my appearance to look more Latina. It was a painful public reckoning in a year of painful public reckonings much bigger than my own.

In the wreckage of the aftermath, I began to recognize that, though the scale of my experience was unusual, the feelings it inspired in me were not. In the ensuing months, I heard from countless people who confessed their reluctance to declare their own identities because, like my grandmother, they're often made to feel they aren't something *enough*. At a book club I visited remotely, one Mexican lady confided that her own sister tells her she's not a real Mexican because she doesn't speak Spanish. Then she rattled off her repertoire of authentic Oaxacan recipes (her sister doesn't know how to cook), and I recognized myself in that moment, too—always eager to preempt accusations of fraud by presenting my *bona fides*. I wanted to reach through my screen and hug her.

Nothing can change who I am, fundamentally. No amount of public derision can undo who my DNA and my family made me to be. The lexicon of identity continues to evolve, and I'll practice using it. Sometimes I will falter, but getting it wrong doesn't make me dishonest. I identify as a human being. A mama. A reader and writer. I identify as my father's daughter. (He didn't much give a shit what people thought of him either.) I know deeply who I am, and I will say it plainly and patiently to whoever wants to listen. Yes, I identify as white because I am white. I also identify as Latina because I am Latina.

I hope we will all get better at this. I hope it won't be even trickier for my daughters, whose father is from Ireland, who drink *coquito* at Christmas, who know where to anticipate "*Nicky Nicky Nicky Jam*" in the Latino pop songs that blare through our house, who prefer *tostones* to *maduros*, and who reapply SPF 100+ onto their pink little noses every two hours when we go to the beach. I will not make it easier on them. I will encourage them to embrace whatever cultural elements of our family feel most resonant, regardless of what anyone might say. In the meantime, while they live in the fleeting, idyllic bubble of their own shared childhood, while they are briefly free to grasp only what brings them joy, if they want beads in their hair? They shall have beads.

Jeanine Cummins is the #1 *New York Times* bestselling author of *American Dirt*. The novel was both an Oprah's Book Club and Barnes & Noble Book Club selection and has been translated into thirty-four languages. Her previous books are *A Rip in Heaven: A Memoir of Murder and Its Aftermath*, and the novels *The Outside Boy* and *The Crooked Branch*. She lives in New York with her husband, two children, and their rescue dog, Joan Jett.

Roses

STEPHANIE DANLER

I keep meaning to write a letter to my children about the rose bush. Since my toddler son, Julian, and newborn daughter, Paloma, were in utero, I have been sending letters to email accounts I set up before they were born. I imagine someday I'll give access to them. The question is: What day will that be?

Sometimes I'm writing to them as they are now (*Mama loves your toothless smile, please don't ever grow teeth*); some when they are a bit older—maybe six? Seven?—and I imagine they'll be curious about their first words (Julian's: car), their birth stories (Paloma: at home in the bathroom). But occasionally I'm writing to my children as adults. I'm trying to tell them about our life right now: the too-small apartment we live in in Silverlake, the walks we take, the concerns we have, the general anxiety of this historical moment. I'm also, it seems, trying to tell them about me. How motherhood changed me and how loving this much unnerves me. That's when the letters give me pause. Where have I gone that I can't talk to my adult children myself?

My mother had a brain aneurysm at forty-six that left her mentally and physically handicapped. I've written about this before. She lost her short-term memory and large swaths of time are gone from her long-term as well. My need to write, to record, predates this tragedy, but my unwillingness to project into the future doesn't. A friend of mine would say to her own baby girl, "We're going to go on so many trips together." "We'll cook so many meals together." When I heard this, I found it startlingly overconfident, bordering on lying. I also wanted to say those things, but haven't found myself brave enough to make unconditional statements. When I held my newborn and whispered to her, it came out, "I'll take you to Italy someday, just the two of us. If I'm around," or "I hope I get to see who you become."

Other parents tell us that we won't remember any of this, the blur of having "two under two," where someone is always crying, where none of us can get all our needs met. And I find myself saying it to new mothers who are sobbing and sweating their way through the milk coming in, the blunt clock of feedings, the hormone drop offs—you won't remember this! I say it though I don't know exactly what kind of consolation that is. Is it helpful to be told that amnesia is a cure for suffering? I won't remember it, and the newborn certainly won't; it's as if that time is erased. There's an unconscious belief that what we can't remember can't hurt us. Having watched my mother, I know that's not true. So I tried, through writing, to remember some of it.

Julian was born in December and the evenings collapsed the afternoons, coming so quickly after the mornings. Around 5 p.m., I would go into the bathroom and weep sitting in the dry tub, not knowing how I would get through one more night. In the mornings the sheets were wet from my milk, his spit up, our tears. Paloma was born at the end of July and our kitchen counters were full of stone fruit. We didn't leave the bed for a week, and she slept easily with some trust or wisdom that she must have inherited from her father. She nursed forcefully while I stared at the rosebush my husband placed directly outside my window. He and Julian got it for me for Mother's Day.

It's funny that I don't have time to write about the rose bush. But I do have time to write a text to my husband asking him to not slam the fridge door because it pops open the freezer door, then everything in the freezer is razed in freezer burn, including my frozen breastmilk, which, though it may be free, is actually something to be conserved.

I have time to make unachievable lists with their perverted idea of productivity and worth, and I have time to text with my sister for forty-five minutes about our children's sleep habits. When I look at how much writing I produce—emails, texts, pitches, outlines, proposals, notecards, scripts, stories—it's not that I don't have time to write, but that I don't have time to figure out what's important. And I don't have time to remember my kids when the reality of them—their physicality and their resounding needs—eats up the days.

I said it was funny, but I think I meant: sad.

I would tell them, if I had time, that roses are foolish in Southern California. They don't naturally thrive in our arid heat, require too much water, fertilizing, pruning, and more attention than we're prone to give. I wonder how my husband knew I wanted roses, despite the work he's put into our drought-tolerant, native-plant-inspired garden. Perhaps he noticed on our walks that I stop for roses, and now Julian does it too, digging his nose into the flower right before he "accidentally" crushes it in his tiny fist. On Mother's Day, it was waiting for me outside the door. It occasionally puts forth a yellow rose, which, for all his prowess in botany, my husband doesn't know are not the most romantic roses. Instead they symbolize friendship, which is what we're banking on at the moment, that our friendship will carry us through these watery early morning wake-ups, and the pandemonium of the dinner, bath time, bedtime gauntlet. What do I really want to say about it? That when I see the roses, I feel loved. I want them to grow to be caring like their father.

Writing to my children isn't only a morbid exercise in instruction for when I'm gone; it's also a time stamp of our world. There are too many firsts, too many developments, and time, since Paloma has been born, has been galloping over me. I see how I will barely complete my sigh and years will go by, and my children will be constantly supplanted and overwhelmed by who they are becoming. I'll never be able to hold on to who they were. It's difficult to describe, but when I write them, I miss them, though they are still easily within my arms.

If I'm around. There are intentional and impersonal abandonments, and both are painful. Where am I going? Will I be leaving the cozy security of this two-parent household for the anarchy of my life before them? Will I be dead suddenly and tragically? Will I be sick, with just enough time, finally, to write these letters? I don't know that any of my writing matters more. My mother was forty-six when she lost the ability to tell me about herself: the way we were as a household of three girls, and who she was beyond the backbone of our lives. I don't know what my first words were, how my mother stopped me from crying, when I first laughed, and I suppose I want to so that I can feel close to her. I'm thirty-seven, and some days forty-six feels around the corner. So I dash off sentences in the middle of the night, and compose longer, complicated stories when I have the minutes. I write as insurance against the uncertainty of our lives. I want my children to know us when we were lovely and it felt like there was so much life still to come. My writing will never be enough, but then I also hope it won't have to be everything.

Stephanie Danler is a novelist, memoirist, and screenwriter. She is the author of *Stray* and the international bestseller *Sweetbitter*. She lives in Los Angeles.

The View Out My Window

JOANNA HERSHON

Over twenty years ago, I was living in an extra-small studio apartment in downtown Manhattan. My life up until then had been dizzy with part-time gigs, acting projects, and brief, doomed relationships. But I'd stopped auditioning and started an MFA in fiction writing at Columbia. The move was not exactly practical, but I was trying to grow up and get to work. And to me—at least while buying time with graduate school—work meant writing my first novel.

During the time I wasn't in class, I planted myself at my butcher-block table, one side of which was pressed up against my studio window, as if the energy from the streets below might somehow make its way into my prose. And I wrote. Or I thought about writing. Or I watched the people and the cars. Or the buildings across the street. The streetlights. The construction scaffolding. Anything else, really, besides the blank page on my laptop.

I was having a little trouble focusing.

To be fair, I was in my mid-twenties and distractions abounded. Should I take an acting job in Massachusetts that I'd just been offered at a theater I loved even though it was a terrible play and I'd just started my writing program? Should I go on a third date with a guy who claimed he was a producer even though I couldn't figure out what he actually produced? Should I go out with the wedding guest I'd recently met who, early in the evening, toasted the bride and groom with a wit so dry it left the crowd slightly confused, and later on sang Elvis tunes (very well!) with the band? I'd been flattered when he asked me to dance. Then we'd drunk too much champagne and made out like two people unlikely to ever see each other again.

The next morning, he'd looked me in the eye and told me to write down my number. We should see each other, he said, while he was in town. Had he mentioned he was living in Mexico? In the July wedding brunch sunlight, his eyes were ridiculously, disarmingly blue. The wedding guest was a very good time, but it hadn't occurred to me that a very good time who lived in Mexico could be anything more than that. I wrote down my number anyway. What did I have to lose?

But when he called the following week, I didn't call him back. In the interim, I'd had a change of heart. Our fun at the wedding seemed like a long time ago, and where could it possibly go? Wasn't I trying to forge a more serious path? He called again, and after the second phone call, I agreed to a drink. By the end of the night, all of my assumptions were turned upside down. He wasn't unserious, he was actually driven. He wasn't flaky, but adventurous and decisive. He wasn't only fun, but he made me laugh very, very hard. By the time he returned to Mexico a few months later, I was hooked.

Now my new boyfriend, Derek, was an accomplished painter. He didn't have a phone or a computer (this was 1997 in rural Mexico so this was not an eccentric choice) and our communication consisted of faxes, which he'd send and I'd return to a mysterious-sounding "*Centro de Mensajes.*" Though I thought of myself as a game traveler, my fantasies ran more along the lines of island hopping in Greece, maybe trekking the moors of Scotland. This town, as far as I could gather, was both a desert and a fishing village, a few days south of California for those who were on the run. I suppose it sounded cool—in maybe a slightly David Lynch kind of way? Whether I liked it or not, I knew I was more of an Anthony Minghella kind of girl. But I really wanted to see him, so when he asked me to come visit over my winter break, I did.

As I exited the plane onto the tarmac I was immediately seduced by the white-hot light. The airport was dusty, hot, with white linoleum floors, and there he was waiting for me: his tan, expectant smile, and a worn blue shirt that matched his eyes and the Pacific Ocean which unfurled out the window on our nearly two-hour drive. The sunset that evening (and every evening afterward) was so pretty that you just had to laugh, it was so absurdly pink. And though the town was crawling with stray dogs and littered with garbage, there were also the ruins of an old sugar mill—sad, but somehow picturesque—plus a deco-era theater and yellow church overlooking a lantern-lined plaza. There were *tacos de pescado* from Victor—handsome and reliably unfriendly—who never changed his fish-frying pace, no matter how many people stood in line. I said a daily *buenos días* to our neighbor Chuy, who was usually planted on his cement porch, playing an out-of-tune guitar. Afternoons brought us to a beach where fishermen in brightly painted panga boats timed their return with the tides. We brought home tuna and tilapia. I picked basil growing in Derek's backyard—an overgrown fusion of cacti, palm, mango, and guava trees with a view of the sea in the distance—and cooked dinners in the Talavera-tiled kitchen while his scruffy dog fetched a mango instead of a ball. For breakfast we slathered our toast with local honey sold in Coke bottles.

Here was one town. And one person. Together they were pinning me down. But instead of feeling restless, I had another thought altogether: *How was I going to recover from this happiness?*

And something else happened. Even though I was supposed to be taking a break from my writing, I wrote anyway. Derek went off to paint (his easygoing lifestyle belied workaholic tendencies) and I'd sit at the heavy wood table and approach a pivotal chapter without doing much hand-wringing. I was once again alone at a table with my writing, but when I looked out the window there was nothing but sky. I was suddenly, shockingly motivated; I simply got down to it.

Maybe it was his offhand manner. There seemed to be little

pressure to do much of anything, and yet we were both putting in full workdays. Derek never seemed to worry if I was having fun, and yet I couldn't remember ever having had such a consistently good time. While I knew that romantic possibility could not make me into a writer, it *was* possible that my recent productivity and sense of balance had something to do with love. By the end of the month, both he and his life seemed inextricable from my own. And as it turned out, he too was ready for a change of scene. We decided to move back to New York together, at least for a while.

Over the past twenty years, I've written the better part of five novels at that heavy wood table in that small beloved town, looking up now and then at the blue sky beyond. We've turned a tool shed into a guesthouse (with no more than many coats of bright paint), and added a much-needed outdoor shower. We gave our children the house's only bedroom and we began to sleep in the loft, which had previously been used for storage. I like it better this way. I like sleeping so close to the *palapa* roof, lying in bed and looking up at the intricate system of palm fronds stitched with leather cords. I imagine each cord as a strand of memory, a braided series of choices.

How, after we'd met at that wedding, could I not have called him back? This thought haunted me for years. How could such a choice have been possible?

Would I have found my writing groove without meeting my husband, without an invitation to fly to a small town in southern Baja, a place I'd never been or thought to go? I certainly think so. But every choice precedes the following one. As I lie in our bed, looking up at those fronds and cords, as I hear the crashing waves in the distance that have become as familiar as honking horns, I've often thought that the sudden clarity I found when I was twenty-five had less to do with the shedding of city distractions or even what we were or weren't doing during those heady months.

I had logged so many hours looking out my New York City window, at the crush of people, at my reflected expectations, that when I found myself looking out a different window that revealed nothing but blue sky—gorgeous, yes, but also a bit monotonous—it was my own internal landscape that changed. I slowed down; I connected.

It was a shift far more radical than I could ever have anticipated.

Joanna Hershon is the author of five novels: *St. Ivo, A Dual Inheritance, The German Bride, The Outside of August,* and *Swimming*. Her writing has appeared in the *Yale Review, Granta, Guernica,* the *New York Times, One Story,* the *Virginia Quarterly Review,* the literary anthologies *Brooklyn Was Mine* and *Freud's Blind Spot,* and was shortlisted for the 2007 O. Henry Prize Stories. She teaches in the Creative Writing department at Columbia University and lives in Brooklyn with her husband, painter Derek Buckner, and their twin sons and daughter.

A Brand New Way

ANGELA HIMSEL

The most difficult thing about writing my memoir was sharing my feelings. Half the time, I didn't know what I was feeling; the other half, I didn't want to share.

My book, about growing up the seventh of eleven children in southern Indiana in a Christian cult and converting to Judaism, came out in 2018. After publication, I spent over a year promoting it, appearing at Jewish Community Centers, synagogues, book festivals, bookstores, and book clubs. In the Q&A after, people often asked me what it was like to convert: Did my parents disapprove? Was I accepted within the Jewish community? The questions, no surprise, were deeply personal. But how could I not answer? If you've already taken your clothes off in public—bared yourself, metaphorically—then why wouldn't you share other personal details, like how you view God today and whether you really feel Jewish inside?

Over time, I loosened up. The more open and vulnerable I was willing to be, the more others felt free to share their stories: Someone's daughter married a non-Jew and planned to baptize her kids; another confessed she attended synagogue every Saturday but didn't believe in God. Turns out, you didn't have to grow up in a doomsday cult to identify with my memoir's central themes: the inevitability of change, making choices, and seeing every shade of grey amid a world that often looks black and white.

I'm happy I wrote the memoir. But I promised myself my next

book would be a novel, something far removed from my twenty-first century American life.

Enter Michal, daughter of King Saul and wife of King David, circa 1000 BCE, Israel. I was reading a semi-scholarly article about King David (because that's how I roll), and in it, a footnote states that Michal is the only woman in the Bible who "loves" a man.

I was intrigued. Why does the Biblical author find it important to mention that Michal loved David? Who is this woman I've barely heard of?

I dove into I and II Samuel and learned she was the daughter of the first king of Israel, and the wife of the second. Michal was at the fulcrum of the creation of the Biblical kingdom many of us remain fascinated by three thousand years later.

After a year of doing publicity for my memoir, I felt a creative void and was anxious to start another book-length project. About what, I didn't know, but I definitely didn't want it to be about me. Then, I remembered Michal and wondered anew why the Biblical authors, who are reticent about expressing emotions unless they entail smiting, deemed it necessary to include "And Michal loved David"? If Michal were the author of her own story, not a footnote in someone else's, what would she say? And that is the genesis of the new, untitled novel I began working on.

Coincidentally, I wrote the first sentence during the first month I moved out of my marital home, my own genesis as a single woman in the first apartment I lived in all by myself. At the age of fifty-eight.

I merrily wrote chapter after chapter. David kills Goliath; David offers two hundred Philistine foreskins as a bride price for Michal; David becomes chummy with his former enemies, the Philistines; David's other wives have children, but not Michal. I created a fictional character, a Canaanite scribe who falls for Michal because, well, I have a thing for Canaanites, and is there anything sexier than a scribe?

About 150 pages and countless hours of research later, I worried that no one except me and an audience of seven Biblical enthusiasts would find Iron Age Israel riveting. Or, maybe the subject matter wasn't the problem? Maybe it was my writing. Sometimes, when faced with these concerns as a writer, you surge past them. Other times, you stew in your doubts. I stewed.

I found myself having a crisis of confidence. What to do?

Revise? Chuck all or part of it? Reimagine it as something else altogether?

All of the above. With real sadness, I tossed several chapters featuring the duplicitous Delilah's fictional lesbian granddaughter. There were only so many Philistines one novel can bear.

And, though the absolute last thing I wanted was to write about myself again, I decided to insert scenes of me shuttling back and forth between my new life and my old one.

Following a revised scene when Michal insists David flee from her murderous father King Saul, I added a chapter of me walking ten blocks from my apartment to my former home, a five-floor brownstone in New York City, where my ex-husband, three adult children, daughter-in-law, delightful granddaughter, three ill-behaved dogs, and the occasional mouse live. I delivered oat milk for my children, helped my ex find his ever-elusive key, sang "Hush Little Baby" endlessly to my granddaughter, and played a rousing game of beer pong with the kids.

I juxtaposed a reimagining of Michal returning to King David after many years, many wives, and a husband apart, with dinner with my new boyfriend. Over candlelight we drank wine and talked about Michelangelo (him) and the Canaanites (me). Late at night, I fell asleep with his legs against mine, his arm around my waist.

At this fork in the road, another writer might create an outline and plot out carefully what this hybrid memoir/novel would be. That writer would not be me. I'm a pantser, not a plotter, and not just in my writing life.

On the contrary. I, too, wondered what the thread is that connects Michal, who was integral to the establishment of the Davidic kingdom, to me, who rules a very ordinary, domestic queendom.

And so I soldiered on to when David brings the Ark of the Covenant to Jerusalem. Michal watches out a window as David jumps and dances lewdly with the maidens. She confronts him with a scathing, "Didn't you just debase yourself in front of everyone?"

To which David responds, "Well, guess what, God chose me, not your father, to be king."

Never taunt a man about his dancing.

She may have once loved David, but I can't imagine this Michal helping David find his keys. Bitter.

The boundary between the past and present, between fact and fiction, is porous. Even though my life bears little resemblance to Michal's on the surface, I imagine she would agree that love is complex. How it begins and endures. Or doesn't. How we change. What we hold onto, and what we let go of. Sometimes things don't work out as we hoped. And, even if you don't have a real plan moving forward, you might have to chuck what you've worked so hard for and reimagine yourself in a brand new way.

🕒

Angela Himsel's memoir, *A River Could Be a Tree*, received the NYC Big Book Award for memoir. Her writing has been published in the *New York Times*, the *Jewish Week*, the *Forward* and others. Himsel studied at the Hebrew University in Jerusalem for two years, earning her bachelor's degree in religious studies from Indiana University. She also holds an MA in creative writing from City College.

Whatever You Write in This Will Belong to You

JEAN KWOK

I was startled awake on my mattress on the floor. I was seven years old and had been deep asleep after a long day at my public elementary school in Brooklyn, followed by helping my family work at the clothing factory in Chinatown until late in the night. I slept fitfully because our dilapidated apartment was overrun with vermin, and I was afraid a rat or cockroach would climb on me, especially since I slept only inches above the cracked vinyl floor.

Had I heard something moving in the darkness of the kitchen? Was it the wind howling against the garbage bags we'd taped over the broken windowpanes? I tried to shift the crushing weight of my covers. I could barely move. I slept under blankets my mother had sewn out of polyester rolls of stuffed animal fur that we had found on the street, discarded by the toy factory. The cloth was neon green, prickly, and backed by thick webbing. It weighed a ton and felt more like carpet than fabric, but that material was a godsend because our apartment didn't have a working central heating system, no matter how hopefully we twisted the radiator knobs. The air was bitterly cold against my face.

Something moved in the darkness. I held my breath.

"Are you awake?"

I exhaled in relief. It was only my brother Kwan, who was ten years older. Like me, he got up early to go to school and then went to work. Like me, he did all of his schoolwork either on the subway or during breaks at the factory. But after my parents took me home at the end of our shift, Kwan and my other brothers went on to a second job waiting tables at a restaurant until two or three in the morning. He must have just gotten home.

He tiptoed past my parents, who were dead to the world on the mattress next to me. They must have just gone to bed. I'd fallen asleep to the familiar sight of my mother working on a sack of clothing she'd brought home from the factory. She always sat next to the oven, which we kept on day and night with its door open, because it was the only source of warmth in our apartment. Her hands would have been too cold otherwise to be able to work. She was so tired. She was constantly nodding off and then jerking herself awake to do a few more pieces before dozing off again. During my entire childhood, I never once saw my mother go to bed before I did.

Kwan laid a package wrapped in brown paper next to me. I gasped. A present! I never got presents. We were the finishers at the factory, which meant that we had to do all of the processing after a garment was pressed. If there was a belt, we had to thread it through all the loops. If there were buttons, we had to do them all up. If there was a sash, we had to turn the sash the right way, then thread it and tie it in a pretty bow. Each garment had to be hung neatly on hangers, and then tagged separately for size, care, and manufacturer. It then needed to be bagged and finally sorted by size on enormous metal racks to be shipped to stores.

For all of this work, we had originally been paid one and a half cents per piece. However, one day, the factory manager had seen Kwan working. He was an extraordinarily hard worker, strong and fast, and she watched him carefully. She understood that he could earn quite a bit more money for us. Instead of praising him or giving him a promotion, she cut the wages for our entire family down to one cent per piece. We'd landed in the United States only two years earlier and were still paying back years of lawyers' fees, visa expenses, and airplane tickets. It took a hundred pieces of clothing to make a dollar. And yet, somehow, Kwan had managed to save enough to buy me a gift.

I touched the package gingerly. I coveted the long-legged blonde Barbie doll another girl at school had, believing the ownership of such a prize would make me long-legged and blonde as well. But I could already tell that this present was the wrong shape. It was boxy, like a book. I didn't mind. Even though I was still learning English and was in the lowest reading group in school, I loved books. I didn't own any.

I was bouncing up and down when I ripped off the wrapping paper. Which book was it? But when I cracked the cover, my heart sank. "Kwan, this book is broken."

"What?" he said, alarmed. All of those hard-earned cents and the book was defective?

"There are no words on the pages," I said, holding it out to him.

He chuckled, relieved. "That's because you're supposed to supply the words. This is a blank journal. Whatever you write in this will belong to you."

I clutched it to my chest, stunned. A place to deposit and explore my own thoughts and feelings! I knew I didn't fit in with the other kids. My brothers cut my hair in a stupid bowl shape, making me look like a boy. I wore clothing my mother made. I spoke English with an accent and didn't understand everything that was said to me. I wasn't allowed to go to other kids' houses for fear that they would then expect to come over to ours. My brothers, who had always played with me back in Hong Kong, were consumed by school and work. And my parents had gone from being parents to being bewildered folks who were even more lost and confused than I was.

It meant everything to have a safe place that belonged only to me.

From that day on, I began to write—in English, which probably helped me learn the language. It wouldn't occur to me for many years to do it for a living. My only goal was to escape the vicious circle of life at the factory. But I felt the pleasure of my pen moving across the page, of articulating my troubles and fears, of understanding that even when something seemed terribly unfair, the very act of recording it would lighten my burden.

That journal has long been lost but I have stacks of diaries that followed it. To this day, I still write in one daily before I begin working on my novels. I've moved so many times and I now live in the Netherlands with my Dutch husband and two kids. But as I run my hand over the tall bookcase in our living room, every shelf filled with translations of my novels which have been published in twenty countries and taught in schools across the world, I marvel that all of this started with one little gift of a journal.

I can imagine how I must have seemed to the other members of my family before that gift: an absent-minded little girl who played with the sheets of ice that covered the inside of our windowpanes during the freezing New York winters. I'd use my bluing fingers to melt small patches, inventing characters spun from ice and daylight. Lost in my own thoughts, I often wouldn't answer immediately when called to help sweep the floor or set the table. I was often chastised for being distracted, but my brother saw me as I truly was: a dreamer and storyteller.

Whenever he saw me writing in my journal, he would smile.

Jean Kwok is the *New York Times* and international bestselling author of *Girl in Translation, Mambo in Chinatown,* and *Searching for Sylvie Lee*. Her work has been published in twenty countries and is taught in universities, colleges, and high schools across the world. Her honors include the American Library Association Alex Award, the Chinese American Librarians Association Best Book Award, and the *Sunday Times* Short Story Award international shortlist. She currently lives in the Netherlands.

Life Lessons, Korean Mother–Style

JENNY LEE

I can admit it: I've spent way too many hours of my life complaining about my Korean mom. Korean moms—and I can only speak about the ones who immigrated to the United States from South Korea and had children born in the States—fall into two camps: the irritatingly helpful and the annoyingly judgmental. The irritatingly helpful KM (the ones who come over to their adult daughter's house and immediately roll up their sleeves, clean the whole place, cook elaborate meals, and are more than happy to help out) has no boundaries, while the annoyingly judgmental KM has standards so lofty not even her perfect future neurosurgeon son could meet them. (A common feature between the two types of KMs is the rote exaltation of anyone with a Y chromosome over their own daughter.)

My own Korean mother falls into the second category. I have a vivid memory of her walking into my first New York City apartment post-college (which I had just cleaned to within an inch of her approval), going over to the television, swiping a paper towel on the black mirror of the flat screen, and presenting it to me. The look on her face was somewhere between "Oh, Jenny" and "Hah! Gotcha." (I am proud to say I didn't cry in front of her. I cried later, while freezing my ass off on the fire escape trying to sneak a cig to calm down.)

I am positive my mother would not remember this incident, and honestly the fact that it still bothers me twenty years later makes me feel somewhat chagrined. As I'm now in my forties and have been adulting pretty hard, I've wondered if it's finally time to get over it. Perhaps it's time to stop complaining about my KM's impossibly high standards and the fact that she brags about the discipline it takes, even now at the age of eighty, to still be able to fit into the same tennis skirt she wore when she was twenty-five, and to just be pleased for her. Yes, she still plays tennis regularly. Which is great. She is in excellent health. Better than my own, I'm sure of it. (For the record, I have a hat that says "WRATH" on it that still fits me from college. So there.)

These days, I've started to challenge myself to look at my KM's hard-core mode of mothering differently. When I find myself thinking back to her litany of complaints when it comes to me—talks too much, laughs too loud, face too round, can't cook, isn't neat enough, etc—I instead ask: How did she shape me into the moderately successful ball of inevitable disappointment I am today? I'll tell you how: with a lot of hard work.

As kids, my siblings and I were under-praised, not overpraised. When my older brother was ten years old, he played competitive tennis on the state level, and I was dragged along to local tournaments. As I hunted for four-leaf clovers in the grass, my KM would use a small pad of paper and log all my brother's mistakes, which she would then go over with him at the end of the match, regardless of victory or defeat. From the sidelines, my takeaways were simple: One, competitive sports were not for me. And two, whenever I needed to offer up my own critique, I would always, always start with something positive first. (Sometimes you learn from doing the opposite of what was done to you.)

When I was twelve, I was second-chair violin in the youth orchestra at the St. Louis Conservatory School of the Arts. I considered this to be pretty good (less glory, sure, but also less pressure), but my KM told me simply that second chair was unacceptable and the only thing standing in my way from being first chair was hard work. I was ordered to practice ninety minutes per day instead of the sixty minutes I had been doing. In her not-so-humble opinion, all I needed to do was put in the time and I would be rewarded (and she would have bragging rights). Of course at this age I believed her. Not once did I ever wonder if the current first chair was more talented than me.

It made no difference that I didn't really care about being first chair, or that I didn't know if I even liked the violin (KMs usually have their children play one instrument and two sports). And it certainly didn't matter that I didn't want to practice for the extra thirty minutes per day. What mattered was having a goal of success and doing everything I could to achieve it—for her *and* for me, so she'd stop talking about it. I never even found out if my efforts worked because we moved to a new city before I had a chance to challenge the first chair to a proper fiddle-off. But I believed she was right (she often told me that she was right about lots of things).

However that wasn't the point.

The point was that I was raised to believe that what stood between me and achieving any goal was simple and quantifiable. It's the sort of magical thinking that has proved invaluable throughout my career as a writer, which like most careers in the arts, is not known for its stability. I'm old enough now to recognize that hard work alone can't get you anywhere you want, but I have two young adult novels; two middle-grade novels; three collections of humor essays; and a career in TV-writing and producing (that I pivoted to in my thirties) to prove otherwise.

Oh, I should mention that my parents were never supportive of my writing ambitions. I had to threaten to skip college altogether to get them to agree to let me go to NYU's Tisch School of the Arts *after* I was accepted early-decision. But because they had instilled in me the determination and skills to do anything I wanted to do, I defied their demands to attend an Ivy League school and become a lawyer and instead used all their sage teachings to pursue what I truly wanted: to be a writer. They were the ones who raised me to believe that I was smart enough to accomplish anything, and I appreciate the work ethic they instilled in me to do whatever it takes to achieve it.

Am I a #1 bestselling author? Nope, much to my mother's disappointment. But hey, who knows? With enough hard work, my mom believes it's still totally possible, and so do I. (Maybe.)

🕒

Jenny Lee is a television writer and producer who has worked on *Boomerang, Brockmire, Young & Hungry,* and Disney Channel's show, *Shake It Up!* Jenny has published two young adult novels (the national bestselling *Anna K: A Love Story* and the sequel, *Anna K Away*) and six other books (crazy, right?!). She lives in Los Angeles with her awesome husband and her giant dog, Gemma, a 135-pound Newfoundland.

Called to the Page

ABBY MASLIN

I am a writer.

Four simple words. Like many writers, however, I've spent decades choking upon them, unable to utter them in clear order without some kind of disclaimer tagged to the end.

I am a writer, but I'm not really trained as one.

I am a writer, but not a real one.

And my default explanation, the one that explains how I've ended up in a sunlit room on the sixth floor of a university building in Halifax, Nova Scotia, having a not-to-be-believed phone conversation with a literary agent while my husband receives speech therapy in the next room: *I am a writer, but only by accident!*

Three months earlier, I'd published an essay entitled "Love You Hard." Simple and unvarnished, it was my testimony to the "Before" and "After" life as a witness to my husband's newly acquired traumatic brain injury. I penned it six months after the random attack that left him nearly dead, adapting to a new normal of physical and cognitive disabilities. At thirty years old, TC's swift loss of independence wrecked me. Each tiny struggle marked by his attempts to form words or walk unassisted signified the incalculable loss we had all suffered.

The essay was easy to write. In fact, I'd written a first version: a more belabored, dressed-up version that I ended up dumping at the last moment in favor of a spontaneously crafted update. The second version, the one that would propel me into the worlds of both publishing and author-dom, was conceived one evening in a small fit of inspiration as I sat taking notes in a graduate school class needed to maintain my license as a schoolteacher.

I was many things in that winter of 2013: a full-time caregiver to my husband, a mother to a two-year-old son, a fourth-grade teacher exercising every benefit of FMLA (Family and Medical Leave Act), and a graduate student earning my second master's degree in order to assume the role of primary breadwinner. In my mind, writers were solely dedicated, holed up in country cottages and rooms overlooking the sea, unweighted by spouses and children and disabilities and criminal court cases. It didn't occur to me, in my incongruous circumstances, that I, too, might be a writer.

Yet from the day of TC's attack, words flowed unfettered from my brain to the computer screen in front of me as I attempted to lasso the language needed to translate my living nightmare. The writing felt urgent: My favorite human on Earth wasn't coming back. I simply could not permit the world to carry on without knowing the full extent of who he was and what he meant to me. I was possessed by heartbreak, a writer's most reliable source of inspiration, and within a few short months, I had composed tens of thousands of words in tribute to TC, the life I actively grieved, and the one I was now attempting to survive.

These primitive blog posts weren't my first foray into writing. From the ages of six through thirteen, I was seized by the act of storytelling: composing plays, poems, books, movie scripts, and everything between. My saintly elementary-school teachers rallied in support of my passion by stepping out of the way and allowing me to write for hours on end. Later they'd hush my peers to give me command of the room while I eagerly read my creations aloud.

Then I went to high school, where it appeared no adult had ever conceived of the idea of encouraging young people to write for enjoyment, and my brief self-identification as a writer ended. I deduced, over the next few years of stiff and smoldering education, that writing was an act that existed in service to other more noble disciplines: science, anthropology, literature. Writing for the sake of writing was quickly forgotten. Only when it became my own form of therapy as an adult was I reminded of its power.

"Do you have anything else I can read?" my soon-to-be agent, Andy, asks that afternoon in Halifax as my boot nervously taps the floor beneath me.

Is she asking out of politeness? Out of pity? I wonder, keenly aware of Andy's obligation to fulfill this phone call as part of the terms of my prize-winning essay. I imagine her sitting behind a mahogany desk in a sleek Manhattan office nearly a thousand miles south of Dalhousie University, where TC and I are participating in a month-long speech-therapy program. That's the thing about having one's life blown up in such a harrowing and ruinous manner: Every act of kindness becomes forevermore tainted by the possibility of pity.

I do, in fact, have something else she could read: twenty-five unedited, unstructured, single-spaced pages of what will later become my published memoir, named aptly after the essay that brought me to Andy.

I almost lie. The very prospect of having Andy's eyes on my crude pages sends waves of nausea through my lower organs. The refrain, *You are not a writer, You are not a writer*, pulses coarsely between my ears.

Someone else speaks, a voice surely not my own. "I do have one chapter I've written."

This phone call will lead to an offer of representation. To a book proposal. To a publishing deal. To the experience of traveling around the country sharing my story. With each milestone, I expect to ditch that ugly refrain: *You are not a writer.* But it continues to lurk, a dogged shadow. I have been uniquely fortunate in my journey to publishing, having drawn the fast pass taking me straight to "Go." My mind, however, is slower to reconcile it all: the transformation to caregiver, then published author.

Circumstances may dictate the roles we play at a given time, but I find comfort in remembering that writing is an unchangeable calling. It precedes and undergirds all the moving pieces of our lives. It may have required my greatest heartbreak to hear that calling once more, but I'm listening now.

Abby Maslin is the author of the *Washington Post* bestseller *Love You Hard: A Memoir of Marriage, Brain Injury, and Reinventing Love*. She is also a public-school educator in Washington, DC, where she lives with her husband TC and their two children. A nationally recognized speaker for traumatic brain injury and caregiving, Abby is an avid yogi and a devout coffee-drinker.

The Circular Breast

SARAH MCCOLL

Today I read that in the first stages of the human embryo, the heart is lodged in the head and only gradually slips down into the breast. I find it a sweet thought that they are born so close together, heart and mind. It confirms my feeling. I usually can't separate one from the other in myself.

—Paula Modersohn-Becker

My first conversation about breastfeeding

An old friend comes to town and we meet in a narrow, airy bar. She drinks two old-fashioneds while I order ginger ale and ask about motherhood. She's no fool but is polite enough not to ask, and I'm still in disbelief of a reality too new and too longed-for to speak of it at all.

There's too much importance placed on breastfeeding, my friend says, to the emotional distress of the mother and physical detriment of the child. She wanted to breastfeed, she says, but she couldn't and her children have thrived nonetheless.

This woman runs marathons and a division of a multinational corporation. I watch rage flash in her eyes, then soften with the second drink, at the shame cast by doctors, nurses, lactation consultants, playgroup moms, and interjecting strangers self-sanctioned to opine on what her body could not do.

Far as I can tell, suffering judgement for one's body, insufficiencies and excesses alike, poisons the cultural core of what it means to be a woman. We laugh like crones. I eat a cherry.

Before this night, I had not imagined any challenges from breastfeeding, and the possibility punctures the heart of my motherhood fantasy born from photographs of my mother in the seventies, long-haired and braless by a river. If I can't nurse my baby, I'd as soon not have one. Alas, too late for this particular insight.

All subsequent conversations about breastfeeding

They ask, *Do you plan to breastfeed?*

I plan to, I say.

Good, they say.

Questions of the artist mother-to-be

I ought to be writing a novel but I type "artist mother" into the web browser. Not as simple as *how to fold a fitted sheet* but a query in search of similar instructional clarity. How will I nurse my twin loves?

I find German artist Paula Modersohn-Becker and her 1906 painting, *Reclining Mother With Child II.* Woman and baby lay on their sides, belly to belly. Their soft, yielding bodies cup together like held hands. *How to nurse and sleep.*

The year after she painted *Reclining Mother,* Paula gave birth to her first child, a daughter, at age thirty-one, and then died eighteen days later of a postpartum embolism. I can't imagine away facts that feel punitive or seem to prove a binary I dismiss. "A pity," Paula said, as she fell to the floor.

Possible answer

I awaken one morning to a book left on my porch by a friend, *The Blue Jay's Dance,* by Louise Erdrich. I have not spoken of my creative concerns, but my friend sniffs them out on the breeze between our houses. Erdrich wades through thigh-deep New Hampshire snowfall to reach her writer's hut, baby strapped to her chest. Baby sleeps, wakes, plays beneath a window.

"One day as I am holding baby and feeding her," she writes. "I realize that this is exactly the state of mind and heart that so many male writers from Thomas Mann to James Joyce describe with yearning—the mystery of an epiphany, the sense of oceanic oneness, the great yes, the wholeness. There is also the sense of a self merged and at least temporarily erased—it is death-like. Perhaps we owe some of our most moving literature to men who didn't understand that they wanted to be women nursing babies."

The pregnant body

Pregnancy books track minute fetal development through the produce aisle from blueberry to cantaloupe. My experience seems tertiary, though it is I who grow these ears and fingernails.

The books don't say what I feel: how my psyche expands with my belly, breasts, and thighs, makes space for another, grows generous enough for the word *mother*. They say nothing of my placid serenity, still as a pond, the bovine contentedness that accompanies my exhaustion, or the quiet, swelling pride in my body's dazzling know-how, a cascade of physical impulses that require no conscious request or reform.

How unlike most experiences in this female form! I am praised for rest, perfect in my lack of effort. Listen to your body, I am told, your instincts, your intuition. *How do you feel?* the world asks, at last conforming to the reality I've long spun for myself, in which all meaningful experience flows directly from this source.

The tectonic shift

My lifelong obsession with the male gaze goes *poof*. I am the subject of my life, object of my interest.

Then another

Early one morning in my second trimester, I awaken to an internal flutter, a bird's flapping wings against my ribs. I am no longer alone in the bed.

To-do list

In my third trimester, I watch a documentary about Toni Morrison. While still working as an editor at Random House, Morrison made a list of everything others asked of her. The list filled a legal pad: call so-and-so, read such-and-such, pay electric bill, buy milk. Then she wrote a list of the essentials, only two items: MOTHER MY CHILDREN and WRITE. I copy each of Morrison's to-dos on an index card and pin them to the center of the bulletin board above my desk.

Rough terrain

I assume it will be easy, that milk will flow as if from a faucet switched on, as easily as I have grown the boy I birth. Turns out there's a learning curve. Nurses and lactation consultants sit bedside. One advises I drop the Virgin Mary posture and hold the baby like a football. Another cuts a hospital bandage into a tube top. You're not supposed to sleep with the baby, she says, but if you sleep with the baby . . . Then she tucks the baby between my breasts, held snug against my skin by the stretchy fabric. We sleep. I bring the tube top home, along with lanolin to rub on my nipples. They crack anyway, and then they bleed, but soon enough, baby and I get the swing of things. I nurse him in the bed, side-lying, our faces curled toward each other, plant and sun.

The circular breast

Years before I was pregnant, when my mother was dying of breast cancer, we sat together one afternoon on the couch. We were having a difficult conversation, the kind eased by side-by-side arrangement. After she died, I wanted to write about what happened that afternoon when we turned toward each other. We embraced and then looked into each other's eyes. That was it, and also not. I wrote the scene again and again, never satisfied. How could I write what I felt in that moment, the energetic tether, the filament strung between us? How could I know what it was I felt, the words fallow and forgotten within me as a dead language, until I nursed my own son?

Sarah McColl is the author of the memoir *Joy Enough*. Her essays have appeared in the *Paris Review*, *McSweeney's*, *StoryQuarterly*, and elsewhere. She is the recipient of fellowships from MacDowell, Millay Colony for the Arts, Ucross, and Vermont Studio Center and holds an MFA from Sarah Lawrence College. She teaches creative writing and lives in Northern California.

I Am the Writer

ARDEN MYRIN

"Congrats, kiddo! MTV wants to buy your show!" I was standing in my TV lit agent's office and he had just informed me that I had sold my first pitch, a dark comedy that I was attached to star in. I was overjoyed. My dream had always been to have a career in the model of Phoebe Waller-Bridge, Tina Fey, or Issa Rae—interesting performers who create their own material.

Even though my primary career up until that point had been as an actress, writing had always been a large part of my identity and something I was very proud of growing up. I had written and staged three plays in high school that I had won awards for. I had gotten an agent at the age of twenty-one from doing stand-up (which I promptly quit because I was terrified of it), and I was coming off four years as a cast member of the sketch comedy show *MadTV.*

The most fun part of being on a sketch show is that as a performer you have a chance to create your own material. In fact, the more you can write for yourself, the better your chance of thriving becomes. So, I dove in, I wrote sketches on my own, and I also collaborated with many of the incredible staff writers. I was a proud member of the Writers Guild of America.

So, back to my TV lit agent's office. He had just delivered the good news, and I was ready to celebrate. Phoebe Waller-Bridge, here I come!

"Wow! That's great!" I said, practically levitating off my chair. "What are the next steps?"

"Well," he paused. "*Who's* going to write it?"

I was confused. Hadn't he just told me that the show *I* had conceived of and pitched had sold? Was he joking?

"I am. I'm going to write it," I said. Duh.

He paused and looked at me condescendingly.

"But *Ardddddennnn,*" he drawled. "We need a *writttterrrrr.*"

And then he proceeded to pair me with a man.

* * *

I am not unfamiliar with having my capabilities underestimated. As a small blonde woman with a high-pitched voice and a playful sense of humor, I have often been dismissed as not intelligent or authoritative. For years, I told myself it was my secret weapon: I could surprise people. But sometimes the digs would get to me.

I have doubted myself in many areas of my life—even after I was cast on *MadTV*. I was self-conscious of the fact that I was not an alumnus of Second City or the Groundlings. Every summer during *MadTV* I would go take writing workshops at the Groundlings, working my way up through their ladder to train to . . . what? Get the job I already had?

On the one hand, I'm grateful that I did the work to educate myself and get better at my craft, but on the other hand I wish I had had the confidence to see that I didn't have anything to prove. There was never going to be a magic moment where I did not feel like a fraud. My brain was always looking for something outside of myself to validate—what? That I was enough? That I belonged? That ONE day would be the day that I woke up and I felt that I could take ownership of my own voice?

Thankfully, I discovered the answer to the riddle, and it was not outside of myself. *I* was the one who had to let me into the club.

Learning to own my voice came by way of an unusual route: I

started to do stand-up again. Not because I was dying to be a stand-up. I felt more comfortable doing improv or sketch where I could play with (and sometimes hide behind) someone else. I started to do stand-up because I needed money.

A little backstory: I was living in New York City, *MadTV* had ended, and I was a regular panelist on the *Chelsea Lately* show. Being on *Chelsea* really started to boost my career. I got to make jokes about pop culture and I was gaining visibility. Almost all of the other panelists were headlining comedians who toured the country every weekend and Chelsea Handler would plug their gigs on the show.

But, financially my numbers were not adding up. It was a late-night show on cable so the panelists made about four hundred dollars a show, and I had to fly myself in (which I was happy to do, it was my choice to live in New York). So basically, on a good week, after agent's fees and taxes, I made about ten dollars.

My friend Bobby Lee, fellow *MadTV* cast member and brilliant comedian, did an intervention on me. "You and I have the same TV credits," he said. "We both were on *MadTV* and we are both on *Chelsea Lately*. This is how much money I make a week touring doing stand-up.[1] You are a fool not to be profiting from this." He was right.

Bobby gave me a little stand-up lesson in his apartment. He taught me the basics about joke structure and thanking the host, but mostly he told me to record all of my sets and listen back, and to hear where people wanted to laugh and I was not letting them.

The thing about stand-up is—yes, there are classes you can take, and yes, you can run your sets for friends—it's really something you have to learn by doing. It's a trial by fire. You just have to jump into the pool and start swimming.

As I followed my comedy Yoda's advice, I listened back to all of my

1 It was a LOT of money. Good for Bobby!!! That little rascal deserves it! He is a comic GENIUS!!

sets and I was shocked. It was not the well-behaved, scripted material that people laughed at; it was my mistakes, my imperfections, and all of the messy sides of myself. *Those* were the parts that the audience loved the most.

It took learning who I really was on stage to help me own my voice off of it.

Since becoming a stand-up comic, I have started a thriving podcast *Will You Accept This Rose?* about the *Bachelor* franchise (but also about grief, because life happened on air and people responded) and I published my first book *Little Miss Little Compton: A Memoir*.

I wrote it all by myself, imperfections, mistakes, and all. It wasn't easy, but I didn't need a male writing partner or any more workshops to make it happen. I just needed to remind myself, again and again: *I* am the writer.

Oh . . . I also fired that agent.

🕒

Actor, author, and comedian **Arden Myrin** was most recently a cast member on the hit Netflix series *Insatiable* and has appeared on over a hundred episodes of *Chelsea Lately, Shameless, Orange Is the New Black,* and *Insecure.* She hosts the podcast *Will You Accept This Rose?* on iHeartRadio, and is the author of the memoir *Little Miss Little Compton.*

Historias Sobre Mi (Stories about Me)

REX OGLE

I was born and raised in Texas. In fourth grade, we moved four times before finally landing in Grapevine. On the first day of school, I entered the playground at recess, quiet and shy and brown-skinned. One kid took it upon himself to ask, "You speak English, spic?" Another fake-sneezed, snorting, "Beaner," under his breath. A third said, "Go back to Mexico, wetback." But when the fight broke out, I was the only one hauled down to the principal's office.

Despite the privilege of having my white father's name, I could not hide the olive skin tones and brown coloring I inherited from my mom. Having dark skin—in the eighties in Texas—was akin to a sin. We Mexicans were somehow less than our white neighbors. So much so, in fact, that my mother told me "never" to speak Spanish—inside or outside our home. Because I was a *quarter* Mexican, and thus only partially a *wetback*, my stepdad thought it rather clever to nickname me "Quarterback."

I never ended up playing football, in part because my mom feared I'd be targeted or hazed for being different. Even my *abuela*, born and raised in Melchor Ocampo, Nuevo Leon, Mexico, wanted me to be cautious. In high school, she warned me, "Do not join any Mexican gangs. They are dangerous, and will ruin your future." Isn't that true of any gang? Why then, with her thick accent and impoverished upbringing on the other side of the border, would my *abuela* specifically call out her own people? I assumed it was because she had received the same indoctrination, the same bad education and misinformation, which of course taught us to fear—if not hate—our Hispanic heritage.

So I steered clear of all things Latinx. I did not celebrate *Día de los Muertos.* I avoided singing the words to "*Feliz Navidad*" around the holidays. I kept away from kids who spoke Spanish as a first language. And when I heard Selena had died in March 1995, I snuck into the closet of my high school's art classroom to cry alone. Even as I was *drawn* to all things Mexican, I did not want to *be* Mexican. So when I filled out employment forms and college applications, I did what I was taught by my family: I checked the box next to the word WHITE.

But in my twenties, I began to dabble. I celebrated *Cinco de Mayo* with margaritas and Tex-Mex. I tried to teach myself *español* (though unfortunately, I can't roll my R's to save my life). I started to collect wedding skeletons and *calaveras.* But it wasn't until my thirties that I began to explore my heritage through the only way I know how: my writing.

I wanted to write a novel about a magical Harry Potter–type hero if he were born in Texas, if he grew up trailer trash, if he hated himself because he was a witch. But as I wrote about my "American Wizard," surrounded by apple pie, monster-truck rallies, beer-bellied rednecks, and the good ole' red, white, and blue, I found something vital missing from my character: his sense of self. Finn Torres has brown skin. His mom and *abuela* were from Mexico. Like me, he was Mexican. But like me, he was clueless about his heritage. So he had to explore. And I began to explore. Before I knew it, as I wrote about my character's upbringing in a world that hated minorities as much as they hated witches, I found myself diving deeper and deeper into Latinx culture.

Like Finn, I wanted to attend a *quinceañera* when I was younger. On my birthday, I wanted someone to wish me *¡Feliz cumpleaños!* I wanted to understand the point of a *Día de los Muertos ofrenda,* with its framed photos, *pan dulces,* yellow marigolds, the *talavera* bowl full of amaranth seeds, the dog *calaca* carved from wood, and the water basin and mirror at the foot of the altar. I wanted to know more about the images of Jesus's mother, haloed by lines and light, and why I've always been attracted to the images of *Nuestra Señora de Guadalupe.* So I watched hour after hour of *telenovelas, películas,* and YouTube clips, not to mention all the days I found myself lost in reading and researching. The more time I spent going down the rabbit hole of my lost heritage, the more I wanted to know.

My middle-grade fantasy novel is still a work in progress. Not because I don't love it, but because my research has evolved into a partnership—I'm not only learning about my magical teen *brujo* as I write, but I'm learning about myself, my family, and the roots I've too-long ignored.

Growing up, I didn't have Mexican heroes in my movies, my cartoons, or my comics. I had white hero after white hero after white hero. But I'm hoping to help correct that. Not just with Finn, but with other strong, resilient, and self-affirmed people of color. My central focus is to create multifaceted protagonists that are like me in all the ways that I am me. I am white, and brown, and Texan, and Mexican. And while I am still working on being proud of all aspects of myself, I am happy to say most of the heroes I create are way ahead of me.

◷

Rex Ogle is the author of *Punching Bag* and the middle-grade memoir *Free Lunch,* winner of the YALSA Award for Excellence in Non-Fiction. Rex also writes under the Hispanic pen name Rey Terciero, creator of the bestselling *Meg, Jo, Beth, and Amy,* and upcoming graphic novels *Swan Lake, Northranger,* and *Doña Quixote.*

To All the Books I Never Sold

ZIBBY OWENS

Before I had four kids, I could write all day uninterrupted. In 2003, I took a year "off" after business school to write a novel, still reeling from recent losses: my best friend on 9/11, my grandfather to leukemia, my step-grandfather to colon cancer, my stepbrother to a drug interaction, and my closest high-school friend to mental illness and suicide via approaching subway. Instead of accepting a job in brand strategy as I'd planned, I decided I could no longer justify spending my days marketing Pepperidge Farm cookies. If I was going to die at my desk like Stacey did in the World Trade Center, I had to be doing something I loved.

My love of writing started in the third grade when I wrote an epic, sweeping story about a set of twins and a magic house. My grandparents, "Gagy" and "Papa Kal," enjoyed it so much they published twenty copies of it as a miniature book on my step-grandfather's printing press. Seeing my name on the spine of that two-inch tome bolstered my determination to become a writer. I would stand on my "Zibby" painted frog step stool in the bathroom I shared with my little brother and recite my acceptance speech for being the youngest published author in history.

I wrote endlessly in journals. Once I learned to type, the words came out even faster, flowing from my fingertips, the conduit to my brain. Somehow, fully-formed thoughts would spill onto the page, thoughts I didn't even realize I was having. Writing became a form of entertainment, self-expression, and therapy.

When my parents got divorced at the start of my freshman year at a new co-ed high school, I gained twenty pounds. People, especially the boys, started treating me differently. A friend told me the guy I had a crush on wasn't interested, but had said, "If she lost some weight, she'd be beautiful." Men on the street catcalled: "Hey, big girl!" I was routinely crushed. I was so upset that I wrote about it one afternoon and printed out my musings on my family's shared printer. Before I could scoop it up, my mother read it.

"Zibby, you have to publish this," she said, clutching the pages in my bedroom doorway. "It'll help so many other girls."

I didn't know the first thing about publishing, so my mother and I looked up the address of *Seventeen* magazine together. We sent it in blind. And they bought it. I still have a copy of that $150 check. I couldn't believe that I could get paid for my words. I went down to the *Seventeen* offices for a photo shoot where the makeup team plucked my eyebrows for the first time ever and stylists posed me holding up a scale in disgust. The piece came out when I was away at a writing program at Bennington College for the summer. My *Seventeen* editor, Rory Evans, told me it had gotten more fan mail than any other recent article. (Thirty years later, Rory is still my editor, now at *Real Simple.*)

Essays were my preferred format. A mind dump in a cute package. I wrote during college and afterwards, for my business school newspaper, for magazines. I interned at *Vanity Fair*, although after about two hours in that job I realized there was no clear path from intern to writer.

At business school, I learned that while my dream had always been to be a writer, my classmates had dreamed of being marketing execs. How could I compete with their passion for a job I didn't really want? So in 2003–2004, I wrote a novel called *Off Balance*. I was so focused on typing all day in my 12th Street apartment that when New

York City's massive blackout happened, I didn't even notice until hours later when I went to print that day's pages.

I told everyone I knew that I was writing a book. I rewrote it three times. First as a memoir, then a novel, then another version, and another, working with freelance editors and a friend from business school, until I dared to show it to a few agents.

While several passed, one agent, Sara Crowe, loved it and agreed to represent me. My hopes were sky-high. We sent it out widely, and . . . it didn't sell. Publishers thought it was "too soon" for a 9/11 story in 2004. One publisher liked my writing style but encouraged me to have the friend die in a car crash and not on 9/11. I was crushed. I gave up after the first eight publishers passed, shoving the manuscript in my desk, forever. I had never failed so publicly at anything before. Every time I saw a friend, they would ask me about the book. Again and again, I'd have to broadcast my disappointment and humiliation.

My agent then paired me up with two women (a fashion designer, Paige Adams-Geller of Paige Premium Denim, and a celebrity fitness trainer, Ashley Borden) who needed a ghostwriter, so I followed up the novel with a fashion and fitness book written in their voices that was published by McGraw-Hill. I got married and had twins.

I kept writing for magazines, for myself, eventually online, sometimes using a pen name. But I constantly felt like a failure. The one goal I'd set—publishing my own book—I couldn't seem to achieve.

After I got divorced in 2015, another agent, Rachel Horowitz, who enjoyed my online parenting essays, followed me on Twitter and took me to coffee. What books did I have in me? She asked. I told her I wanted to publish a collection of essays as a book called *Moms Don't Have Time to Read Books*, but she said I had "no platform" and didn't think publishers would find the title funny. A new friend suggested I start a podcast. I figured, why not? I used the rejected book title and got to work interviewing authors.

Meanwhile, I wrote another book called *Forty Love,* about falling in love again at age forty (with a tennis pro), first as a memoir, then a novel, and then I rewrote it again. Again and again. I got another agent, Joe Veltre, after Rachel went back to the publishing side. My platform had grown, thanks to *Moms Don't Have Time to Read Books.* So I tried to sell a new book of (unwritten) essays called *Happy Sad Happy Sad,* about all the things I didn't think I had time for that ended up changing my life. All the publishers we tried passed, some even meeting with me and seeming very enthusiastic. One editor emailed my agent to say, "We loved it. More news tomorrow!" And then passed. I was once again crushed. I found out about the final rejection when I was in London where I'd traveled to accept a Lovie Award for my podcast. I sobbed on the bathroom floor in the middle of the night. All I wanted to do was write a book. My one dream! Every day I sat and talked to people who had achieved their goal. Why couldn't I? I knew I had something to say that others would appreciate hearing.

I doubt myself in many areas (don't even get me started about my body issues), but I know that I can write. I need to write. I live to write. No, I'm not a literary novelist, and I won't be winning the National Book Award, but I've always been able to get through to people on a deeper level with my words.

Meanwhile, I still wanted to sell *Forty Love.* I packaged it with a cute little Z-shaped ceramic tray filled with mini tennis balls and sent it to five publishers . . . on March 11, 2020. The very next day pandemic life began. We fled New York City, which quickly became the epicenter of the coronavirus, and my manuscript languished on abandoned desks for months. I followed it up with digital versions, but those publishers still passed. Some wanted another thirty thousand words. Another wanted shifts in the timeline. More details. Enhanced characters. Revisions. I'd written it on airplanes, in doctor's waiting rooms with my kids hanging off my shoulders, on the playroom floor, in bits and pieces, before daylight, after bedtime, whenever I could find a spare minute. And yet, another rejection. I couldn't even bear to incorporate the conflicting suggestions I'd gotten in the midst of quarantine times, so I abandoned the project, throwing myself into helping authors whose books were launching. If finally releasing a book was as much of a dream come true for them as it would have been for me, I wanted to help them celebrate and enjoy their moment.

Along the way, somehow, I did end up selling two children's books. An author I'd had on my podcast, Karen Dukess, introduced me to her friend, an editor who was starting her own children's book imprint at Penguin Random House. On the day of our meeting, my daughter had to stay home from school sick. I was about to cancel when my husband suggested I just invite the editor, Margaret Anastas, over for lunch.

"Here?!" I asked.

"Why not?" he said. "Maybe she'd like to get out of the office. Who knows?"

Margaret accepted my invitation within minutes.

At my dining-room table, over chopped salads and counting our Weight Watchers Points, Margaret pulled out her phone and showed me an illustration of a girl.

"Her name is Princess Charming," she said. "If you were to write a book about her, what would it be about? Want to take a stab at it?"

"Sure," I said. "Why not? Let me think about it."

We went back to our salads.

Two minutes later I put down my fork and said, "OK, here's what I would do."

Margaret loved the idea.

"Do you know how to write a children's book?" she asked.

"I mean, I've written a few for fun, but not really," I admitted.

"Do you have a piece of paper?"

Margaret sketched out the page boxes and taught me how to

structure the story. It only took three quick drafts and I had a contract in hand for two books.

I also ended up taking a collection of essays I'd commissioned during the quarantine and turning them into an anthology, *Moms Don't Have Time To: A Quarantine Anthology.*

My teenage son said recently, "But you didn't *write* the anthology. How is it *your* book?"

It wasn't. It isn't. (And neither, really, is this one in your hands now. Not in the way that mattered to me.) To be honest, despite producing these anthologies, hosting two podcasts, editing an online magazine, and hosting a virtual book club, I sometimes still feel like a total failure. I haven't sold the book I want to write, but, having interviewed over six hundred authors in the past three years, I've definitely gotten some fabulous writing advice. And I've accidentally discovered my passion for having intimate conversations via podcast, and even building my own brand, Moms Don't Have Time To.

My grandmother, Gagy, passed away recently at age ninety-seven. She read all the drafts of my unsold books and novels, but never got to hold a finished, published book written entirely by me in her hands. Not even an anthology. And now she never will.

But I won't give up. I'm still that little girl on the step stool wanting to be a real writer with a book all my own. Ironically, when the first anthology came out on February 16, 2021, I was struck by COVID days before. I did my book tour events from bed in between naps, dizzy spells, fever, and coughs. Guess what I used to prop up my laptop on my legs? That very same step stool.

I hope I can pull it off one day. I know for sure that I won't stop trying; I'm a writer and this is what I do, even if I don't have the proof just yet. And when I do, I know that Gagy and Papa Kal will be watching from above. Cheerleading from heaven until *the end.*

Note: Several months after writing this essay, I did it!!! I sold a memoir proposal to a publisher! I can't explain how amazing it felt to have achieved something I'd been trying so hard to accomplish for my entire life. The Book Messenger will be published by Little A, an Amazon Publishing imprint, in July 2022. Stay tuned!

Zibby Owens is the creator and host of the award-winning podcast *Moms Don't Have Time to Read Books.* She is a regular contributor to *Good Morning America* online and the *Washington Post*, and her work has appeared in *Real Simple*, *Parents*, *Marie Claire*, *Redbook*, and many other publications. She lives in New York with her husband, Kyle, and her four children.

The Reason Behind the Words

CLAIRE BIDWELL SMITH

On a date with my first husband I told him that I didn't want to have children. We were walking across a bridge in Chicago's Grant Park and it suddenly struck me what a wonderful father he would be. "I want to write books and travel the world," I told him. "There won't be time for those things if I have kids."

He simply nodded, a mysterious gleam in his eye, as if he knew something I didn't. And just like that, fifteen months later we were married and, you guessed it, expecting our first child together. Chalk it up to biology or foolishness, whatever the case—I was about to go over the waterfall into parenthood and I felt an acute sense of panic that I had not yet written a book.

I had been a writer for as long as I could remember, scribbling out stories about ladybugs and fireflies as soon as I could put a pencil to paper. As a teenager, I'd been the school poet, and in college I'd majored in creative writing and followed that with an early career working for a series of glossy magazines.

I came by all the reading and writing honestly. I grew up an only child, and a lonely child too, the daughter of two much older parents. With no other siblings, my childhood was spent reading books at the dinner table while my parents swirled martinis and talked politics. Books became my companions. I read on the school bus and in the car. I read at breakfast and at night, under the covers with a flashlight. By middle school I was not only reading stories but writing my own as well. Soon, writing became my sole way of making sense of the world.

I was fourteen when my parents both got cancer within months of each other, and books and writing became my lifeline. It was as if I had been priming myself all this time for this experience. Now I read books in the hospital waiting rooms, and late at night, in bed with a flashlight, I wrote long poems about my mother's cancer, the pain in my father's eyes.

But wait . . . back to that first husband. My parents both died, as you might suspect. It seemed as if I had set myself up for tragedy with all those dreams of being a writer. And ten years later when I walked through that park in Chicago with the man I would marry, I felt certain that I wouldn't—and couldn't—have children because I hadn't yet written the books I always knew I would write.

But just as death has its plans for us, so does life. At age thirty-one, married with an infant daughter asleep in my lap, I reached across to the keyboard and that book I'd always dreamed of writing poured forth. I had to laugh—after all those years of sitting and planning and reading and writing, now that I was immersed in motherhood and diapers and no time at all it seemed I could do nothing *but* write.

I wrote in my sleep, waking up with the words in my head. I scribbled them out while I nursed the baby, and I said them aloud as I drove to my job as a grief counselor at a snowy little hospice in the north suburbs of Chicago. Death was everywhere then, but so much life too. The lives of the people left behind. Of me and the granddaughter my parents never got to meet, the lives of the people I sat with at kitchen tables who hung their heads and wept for the people they had lost, it was all muddled together in a great, gasping breath of existence.

And I could see it now in a way I never had, and I could do nothing but write it all down.

My first book was published the same year I became pregnant with my second daughter. We were living in Los Angeles by then, amid the palm trees and the hazy boulevards that stretched toward the ocean. The book was out in the world, but there was still more to say, and even less time to say it. In that same way you might know that you will have another baby, I knew I would write another book.

The days and weeks puddled out around me like sand in an hourglass. My marriage was falling apart; we were broke with two children living in a bungalow in Santa Monica. Yet still, all I could do was write.

Over the course of ten years, from age thirty to forty, I wrote three books and gave birth to three children. There was also a divorce and a second marriage. There was never any time, and there was also all the time in the world. I'm nursing a baby as I write these words, his legs draped across my lap, one warm little hand on my chest, and my arms outstretched to the keyboard. I've been doing this for so long—writing through motherhood, writing around it, and writing because of it. The feeling of time bleeding out is so present.

When people ask me if I'm surprised by all the books I've written and the success I've achieved in my career despite being a busy mom, I always laugh and shake my head. No, I tell them. I'm not surprised by the books; I'm surprised by the kids.

Yet, I realize now that it's the kids that created the time to write that I didn't think I had, because they are the reason behind the words. They are the hope and the urgency that drives my fingers across the keyboard.

Claire Bidwell Smith is a therapist specializing in grief and the author of three books of nonfiction: *The Rules of Inheritance, After This: When Life Is Over, Where Do We Go?* and *Anxiety: The Missing Stage of Grief.* In addition to having given dozens of talks on grief, Claire has written for and been featured in many publications including the *New York Times, The Atlantic, Goop, O, The Oprah Magazine,* and *Psychology Today.*

Clarity Arrived

LAURA TREMAINE

I turned in the manuscript for my first book just three weeks before the coronavirus pandemic brought the nation to a standstill in March 2020. The publisher returned it to me needing extensive edits the very same week that my hometown of Los Angeles entered a strict lockdown. After years of spending my weekdays working alone in introverted heaven, my two elementary-aged children were suddenly at home screeching into their Zoom screens. My movie-director husband was housebound, yelling contingency plans for his latest project onto conference calls. I sat upstairs in our home office, staring at a Word document full of red corrections and commentary, and gripped the sides of my desk with white knuckles.

This book had been over a decade in the making. I started a mommy blog when my daughter, now eleven, was still soft and pink and breastfeeding, with the dream of one day holding a book with my name on the cover. But the publishing industry is elusive and fickle, and it took me years of stops and starts, rejections, and mediocre ideas before I finally learned to write for an audience. My mommy blog led to paid writing gigs, then to podcasting, and eventually to an agent who helped me craft a book proposal using my years of experience sharing stories online.

So when I finally landed a book deal, I was cautious and superstitious, and I built a lot of myth and magic into my subsequent writing process. Before I turned in that first draft to my publisher, I drove out to the desert (twice) to write the hardest sections. I left my family for a week at a time to write in a house in the woods, like a fantasy of what I thought "real writers" did. I depended on silence and solitude to form the sentences that would forever be My First Book.

But when my manuscript was returned to me for edits just days into the pandemic, all the ritual and pomp I'd created for my writing was obliterated. I had no choice but to do this work with my young children underfoot and the world in crisis.

It wasn't just a writer's fantasy that made me believe I could only work under certain conditions. Managing a lifetime of acute anxiety means that I build walls around routines and productivity. It makes me feel safe to have A Way To Do Things, and I function better as an adult, spouse, and mom when I know what to expect and what is expected. Of course, as the pandemic swept the globe, no one knew anything. It was terrifying and panic-inducing.

And yet, my final deadline loomed.

Editing and rewriting was slow going, but what else did I have to do? Everyone's schedule was cleared. If "time" was a gift of this forced quarantine, we were drowning in it, because the initial Los Angeles lockdown was apocalyptic. For months, everything non-essential was closed. We were told not to leave the house unless absolutely necessary. When I did venture out to the grocery store, I returned near tears. The lightness that L.A. is known for was replaced with a pervasive dread. People standing in line to buy milk and frozen pizza weren't smiling behind their masks. The stores turned off their elevator music, leaving these cavernous spaces with empty shelves and silent shoppers. Every essential errand left me depleted and fearful.

After a few weeks, I had no choice but to return to the book. As a first-time author, the editor's notes were confusing. I wanted the book to be better, but reshaping every chapter was daunting. Even under the best of circumstances, I would have struggled with the task. And these were not the best of circumstances. The kids needed a snack. The internet glitched with four people on it all day. The COVID-19 statistics mounted. I had every excuse to ignore the rewrites, but I just couldn't stomach asking for an extension.

So I slowly worked on one section, and then another. I set a timer on my phone for thirty-minute intervals and rewarded myself with chocolate after two hours of work, regardless of how much I'd gotten done. I learned to concentrate on one paragraph at a time even when the kids were dribbling a ball in the living room during "remote P.E." My anxiety eased with these new rituals. It wasn't the disciplined, Zen writer life that I had always pictured, but the pages started to come together.

Over and over the main note from my editor was about clarity. *Be more clear here. What does this mean? How does this relate to the main point?* I closed the door and turned off the WiFi and focused on that message alone: Get clear. And as I wrote my way to clarity, clarity started to appear. The effects reverberated off the page: I removed people from my social-media feeds and deleted items off my to-do list. In every aspect of my life, I began to ask how it related to the main point, and anything that was unclear had to go. The sentences in my book got stronger, and so did I.

At one point, finishing my first book in a pandemic seemed unthinkable, yet still I did just that. I learned the advantage of a deadline, the freedom in releasing a fantasy, and the power of a thirty-minute timer. My editor forced me to make my book's message super simple, and that clarity brought everything else into focus.

My next book is due in late 2021. It will be a bonus if I'm able to make it out to the desert or the woods to get some work done. But if I can't, I can't. The most important thing I've ever written was created under duress, with frequent interruptions, and not a speck of quiet.

When I listened for it, clarity arrived.

Laura Tremaine is a writer and podcaster in Los Angeles. Her first book is *Share Your Stuff. I'll Go First.*

MOMS
DON'T HAVE
TIME TO
LOSE WEIGHT

I Diet, Therefore I Am

ELYSSA FRIEDLAND

Last March, just before the world turned upside down from COVID-19, I was at a party with my husband. New York City was teetering on the edge of normalcy. We weren't hugging or kissing our friends, but we were still chatting with them in indoor spaces and even dancing—albeit awkwardly and with elbow bumps. I was dressed in a brand-new orange satin skirt, silk tank top, and four-inch heels. But instead of enjoying the party—what would ultimately be the last normal experience I would have for the foreseeable future—I was worried about my appearance.

Did I look chubby? Why didn't I skip dinner the night before, knowing I had this party? Should I try that ridiculously expensive stomach-tightening machine at the dermatologist again? She said the third time might be the charm. I looked around the room at the other partygoers. The woman in the strapless black dress had an incredibly toned body, but she didn't work outside the home like I did, so she probably had more time for the gym. Another person I recognized looked like a size double zero in her winter-white pantsuit (imagine, being able to wear white without Spanx!), but I reminded myself that she was a good ten years younger than me. I couldn't help it—the compare-and-despair dance was a habit as practiced as my drink order (vodka soda with a twist of lime: low-carb and low-cal).

For most of my life I've been a fairly healthy weight. I live within a fifteen-pound bandwidth. What vacillates far more than the actual number on the scale is my mood associated with it. A "low" number puts a spring in my step for the entire day. A "high" number makes me cranky and rude to everyone in my path—and I avoid mirrors at all costs, sometimes taking a circuitous route to leave my own apartment.

There's almost always some event or milestone driving my weight-loss plans. A bar mitzvah. A vacation. A big birthday. These events keep me out of the kitchen as I pine for pints of Ben & Jerry's and fantasize about hopping in the deep fryer with the French fries. But everything changed when coronavirus descended upon the world like a social chastity belt and suddenly there were no more events for the foreseeable future. My calendar was wiped clean.

I clicked delete on the soirées that would have previously zipped my mouth shut. I canceled hotel reservations in locations that called for bathing suits and tank tops. My first thought as the reality of the new normal set in was that now I had the freedom to get fat. I should have been thinking about the overcrowded hospitals, the refrigerated morgues, and children forced out of school. Instead, I thought about cake.

I went on FreshDirect and began the process of hoarding all the sweets I normally denied myself, along with toilet paper and Lysol. Cartons of ice cream, bags of Oreos, tubes of Pringles, and sweating wedges of cheese arrived at my doorstep. I imagined spending the next few months seeing no one but my family, wearing elastic waist pants, and finishing Netflix series, all while double-fisting highly caloric foods.

But when my groceries arrived, a surprising thing happened: After about two days of indulging, I found myself at an impasse. I didn't want to try the ice cream in my freezer. The boxes of Girl Scout cookies standing like soldiers in my pantry weren't crying out to me.

I was stalled, but not by the pressure to appear attractive on social media. My plan to eat feverishly as though dessert was going out of style was foiled by my own vanity: I feared the numbers creeping up on the scale, even if I didn't dare weigh myself. My id was begging for chips, but my superego forced my hand to salad.

The counterintuitive experience reminded me of a Mother's Day project my daughter brought home in nursery school. She had to fill out a questionnaire with my favorite things. Favorite hobby: reading. Check. Favorite vacation: Hawaii. Another check. Favorite food: salad. *Hmm.* If I had to list my favorite foods in order from one to a hundred, salad would place somewhere in the high nineties. But I eat it all the time, which explained my daughter's answer. The line between a genuine like and a habit was blurry at best.

At what point were we even dieting anymore? I wondered. If I'm always watching what I eat, so much so that I can't even relax during a period of total isolation, then do I even exist as a separate entity apart from the diet? Or has the diet become a part of me as fixed as my eye color?

But there was a bright side to the inability to let myself relax during quarantine: It led to a breakthrough in self-awareness. I realized that I didn't just count calories because I wanted to appear hot and sexy to others. I actually desired fitness and thinness for my own self-satisfaction. So why wasn't I happier?

These worries niggled at me until the weather turned and I was able to do more outdoor activities safely. I went back to playing tennis on occasion. I did some jogging with my daughter. I took long walks on the beach. And it hit me, sometime in July right after I celebrated my thirty-ninth birthday. I wasn't unable to pig out because I was desperate to be thin. I chose to eat well because I felt better when I did. I was craving salad because when I put vitamin-rich, natural foods in my body, I had more energy to play with my kids. My husband even says I'm less cranky.

I don't want to sound too corny or fake. I still want a killer body (though three pregnancies have made that goal practically obsolete).

I still want to walk into a party (remember gatherings?) and feel sexy. But that's only a part of the bigger picture.

I know myself better than I did in March 2020. I'm not this repressed woman denying herself chips. I'm a reasonably well-adjusted woman who knows life is about balance. Mondays can be for cake but then Tuesdays should be veggies. Wednesdays can be elastic-waist sweats but Thursdays should be zippers and buttons. It's a better example to set for my children. It's the better way to live.

When COVID-19 is behind us, you will find me in the grocery store with a cart full of healthy foods and that front section filled with more indulgent snacks. I'm not quitting carbs forever. And I'm not going to live on carrot sticks. I'm going to live my life and do what feels good, for mostly all the right reasons and a sliver of vanity mixed in.

It's all about balance—just like a large, leafy salad with full-fat dressing on top.

◷

Elyssa Friedland is the author of four novels. Her latest book is *Last Summer at the Golden Hotel.* She lives in New York City with her husband and three children. A graduate of Yale University and Columbia Law School, she also teaches creative writing at Yale.

Peloton and On and On

RICHIE JACKSON

I blame my weight problems on my husband. Seventeen years ago when we met, I was twenty-three pounds overweight (which in gay weight is seventy-five pounds) and he still fell in love with me. Over the course of our relationship and my constantly fluctuating waistline, he's never mentioned it once. He doesn't raise an eyebrow when he catches me shoveling spoonfuls of ice cream into my mouth straight from the container in front of the open freezer, nor does he mention the collection of pants in our closet with varying degrees of waist sizes that I always keep on hand. We don't make love any less when I am a size 34 than when I am a 30. For seventeen years, I have chosen to see me the way he sees me.

So in 2016, when Donald Trump was elected and I was eating with abandon because I was so angry at all his lies and attacks on the LGBTQ community, it took my doctor at my annual physical to point out that I had gained twelve pounds since my visit the previous year. My response, thinking of course he'd understand, was: "Well, Donald Trump . . . " But his unhelpful prescription was only: "Get a hold of yourself."

I couldn't get over a trusted medical professional using such accusatory language as if my ballooning stomach—which by now looked like I was carrying a tire around with me—was simply a result of my being lazy. By this time, I had enough therapy to know that I had once again fallen into my own self-sabotaging trap. Once again, I was numbing myself with too much food and too much wine, my savory enablers. I should have known better—all the other times I had gained weight in my life had been in response to grief, sadness, and terror.

When I was a first-time expectant father, our twin boys were born three months premature. Our firstborn died and our son Jackson hovered near death, battling mightily in the NICU for three months until we were able to take him home. A year later, my oldest sister died of cancer and a year after that, my then-long-term relationship ended. My life was a tsunami of misery. For the three months our son was in intensive care, I ate burgers and drank beer at lunch and dinner every night. When my sister died and my fifteen-year relationship imploded, it was takeout Chinese food with three glasses of wine nightly. I didn't want to get drunk, I just wanted to get tired enough to go to sleep so the day would finally be over. To say I ate and drank my feelings would be an unforgivable understatement.

On March 13, as we headed into sheltering in place for COVID-19, I was already at a size 34 and climbing. Having lived through the AIDS epidemic in the 1980s when I was in college, I knew what was coming for us: disease, death, fear, grief, anger, helplessness. I vowed to myself that I would finally break out of my vicious cycles of emotional avoidance and work hard to confront everything directly. Even though I'd be socially distant from family and friends, I'd make sure not to social-distance from my own feelings. I know what a silent tormenter grief is. If you aren't aware of it, don't treat it, and don't confront it, it will spread like a cancer. I vowed I'd grieve properly all the loss and sadness around me: the death and illness of friends and fellow citizens, the demise of our democracy, my elderly parents imperiled, our son's college-freshman experience ruined.

To get through this pandemic I needed to stay keenly aware of my feelings and stay healthy so as not to slip back into the pints of Haagen-Dazs or bottles of chardonnay. And as the pandemic raged on, I wasn't only challenged by my own feelings, but also as a spouse and parent. I had to help manage the emotions of my husband and children as well, which over the course of nine months (and counting) in isolation together, fluctuated daily. While one morning one of us would wake up hopeful, another would feel hopeless. To help me, I started journaling again—it was a relic of my teens that helped me stay aware of everything and gave me space to sort out my feelings.

This was all particularly challenging because while sheltering in place, I didn't have any time for myself. I was literally never alone. My husband no longer went to an office; our youngest son's preschool was now on Zoom; and our older son, who had gone off to college, moved back in—his classes now were all remote.

I found myself craving privacy, desperately. So I turned to our year-old, unused Peloton bike. I did the math: thirty minutes for a class, ten minutes to shower. Surely I could extract forty minutes in the day just for myself. While the world was being ruined, exercise might have seemed frivolous and privileged, but again I leaned on my experience from the AIDS war; taking care of yourself is a sacred obligation so that you can be healthy enough to take care of others.

I settled into a daily routine and one-sided monogamous relationship with my go-to Peloton instructor, Cody Rigsby. He seemed as invested in my progress as I was, so now I had a sponsor of sorts. Class after class, Cody implored me to dig deeper and work harder. He pointed out that if I can withstand being uncomfortable during our ride together, I can withstand uncomfortable situations elsewhere. I was never one who felt better after working out; I never got a rush of endorphins, but now I was feeling invigorated by my regimen and so protective of my alone time I never missed a day. Cody was giving me the fortitude to confront what was happening to all of us, his constant reminder to "trust and believe in yourself" became my mantra on and off the bike.

And as of September 3, 2020, 128 Peloton Cody classes later, I had lost twenty-three pounds. I was solidly in the size 30 pants zone and had found a strength and resilience I hadn't known I was capable of. And yes, finally, I got a hold of myself.

I will do it again tomorrow, and the day after that, and on and on.

Richie Jackson is the author of *Gay Like Me: A Father Writes to His Son*. He is an award-winning Broadway, film, and television producer whose recent projects include Harvey Fierstein's *Torch Song* and Showtime's *Nurse Jackie*. He lives in New York with his family.

Mama, Am I Pretty?

JEAN KWOK

On the morning of my elementary-school graduation, I stared at myself. My family had done their best. The combined efforts of my well-meaning brothers and my conservative mother, all recent Chinese immigrants who were absolutely clueless about what was considered attractive in Brooklyn, had led to this image in the pockmarked mirror: My short frizzy hair, cut at home, puffed out above an ill-fitting cowgirl dress that sagged on my petite frame, complete with *faux*-leather vest and sticky plastic boots. My silent mother stood behind me and finally, on this day when I wanted so much to look good, I blurted out the question I'd been afraid to ask for many years.

"Mama, am I pretty?"

My mother hesitated. I could feel the words cycling through her head. She didn't want to hurt me. Finally, she sighed and said, "It's just that you're so skinny." Seeing the devastation on my face, she quickly added, "At least you have nice eyebrows."

She wanted a tall, plump daughter and I was thus a disappointment in every way. My mother had been considered one of the most beautiful women back in our village in China: fair skin against dark hair, gentle and rounded as a soft rice ball dusted in powdered sugar. I took after my darker skinned father, all sharp knees and elbows, a scrawny sticklike child with a lollipop of a head.

In our family, there were no affectionate hugs or I-love-you's. Instead, food was an expression of love, and of hope. As the youngest of seven children, I stood on the lowest rung of the power hierarchy, but I was still the baby. While my older brothers stood behind us to eat, my parents and I sat down at our small rickety table for meals. With their chopsticks, my family would fill my rice bowl with the choicest morsels—hunks of pork belly, water spinach, marinated chicken claws, steamed fish eyeballs, and fermented tofu. To make things worse, we were very poor and struggled to even pay the rent. My parents and older siblings had fled from China to Hong Kong, where I was born, and made the leap to the United States when I was five years old. They had known hunger. The problem was I was a Chinese kid who hated Chinese food.

We were living in a dilapidated apartment that was overrun with vermin and didn't have a working central heating system. It was bitterly cold in the winter and I spent much of my childhood being sick. My nose was rubbed raw from constant colds, so much so that my teachers stared at me because of how chapped the skin was on my face. My family toiled in a clothing factory in Chinatown and every day after school, my father brought me there to work as well. I spent my life shuttling between the freezing apartment and the factory, where I struggled to breathe through massive clouds of fabric dust. We left at around nine or ten o'clock in the evening, and after getting home, my mother would still need to cook. Sometimes it was almost midnight before dinner was ready. After long days at the factory, the adults must have been starving, but often I could barely keep my heavy eyelids open, especially since I had to get up early for school the next day. I only wanted to go to sleep.

My family couldn't understand this. Refusing food was like averting your face from a kiss. I was told in no uncertain terms that to be skinny was to be ugly. Spoiled and ungrateful. Secretive. Shallow. Pretentious. Stupid. Every meal, I sank deeper and deeper into my seat as everyone glared at me. I mentally divided my white rice into quarters so that I could shovel it into my mouth and force myself to swallow. My heart sank whenever another piece of food landed in my bowl.

"You're on a diet," my brothers would say accusingly while I didn't even know what a diet was. "You are becoming like those Americans who think they're too fat. The next thing you know, you'll be lying in the sun to become even darker."

For them, only working-class laborers were skinny and dark. When I didn't eat much, they believed I had adopted Western standards and was betraying our customs and heritage. I grew to hate mealtimes. It became a vicious cycle. The more they berated me, the less I wanted to eat. To be fair, their insistence stemmed from worry for me. My mother wanted me to become tall and strong, to thrive in this new country. Her solution was to fatten me up by any means possible.

She became great friends with the man in the medicine store, who made announcements like, "Mrs. Wong's daughter ate this and grew as fat as a pig."

"Wrap that up for me," my mother would answer.

At home, my mother would carefully boil down the expensive and rare ingredients into a tiny, bitter cupful, which I would then be required to consume: salted crushed bumblebees, shavings of deer antlers, nameless vile herbs. This did not encourage me to consider food in a more positive light. And nothing changed my weight.

Let me be clear: Now that I've had two kids and live a sedentary life as a full-time author, being too skinny is not a problem. I have spent most of my life immersed in Western media, food, and attitudes. Like many others, I too worry about those extra pounds and getting enough exercise to compensate for all the chocolate I eat for inspiration. I've come to understand that I was never too thin as a child either. I never had an eating disorder. I was never outside of healthy weight boundaries. It saddens me that to the day she died, my mother never thought I was pretty based on her own culturally ingrained definition.

But, after growing up in a country with a very different perspective regarding weight, I've learned how arbitrary any judgment regarding our bodies is. Whether society tells us we're too thin or too heavy, the end result is the same: shame and blame for anyone who doesn't fit the rigid mold. That realization has freed me in many ways.

These days, I'm happy with the way I look and I've learned not to care what anyone else might think. When I eat, I enjoy everything from Indonesian rijsttafel to sushi. I even love Chinese food.

And as I look back on my childhood of forced mealtimes and potions from the pharmacist, I see it all a bit differently now. My family wasn't trying to change me; they were trying to help me take up space in the world. I understand that if food was the currency of love, I was rich indeed.

Jean Kwok is the *New York Times* and international bestselling author of *Girl in Translation, Mambo in Chinatown,* and *Searching for Sylvie Lee.* Her work has been published in twenty countries and is taught in universities, colleges, and high schools across the world. Her honors include the American Library Association Alex Award, the Chinese American Librarians Association Best Book Award, and the *Sunday Times* Short Story Award international shortlist. She currently lives in the Netherlands.

The World I Build for You

BROOKE ADAMS LAW

Dear Jacqueline,

On picture day in seventh grade I wore a red velvet-trimmed V-neck camisole with a matching cardigan. I blow-dried my hair straight and (I hoped) shiny. I went to a Catholic school where we normally wore uniforms, so picture day felt special.

All day long—in the lunchroom, in the library—I noticed that boys were calling my name, then laughing and ignoring me when I turned around. Finally my friend Kevin told me that they just wanted to stare at my chest.

Apparently my breasts were larger than most of the other girls'. I had never noticed.

"You shouldn't wear shirts like that," Kevin said. "It'll make people think you're like *that.*"

My other friend Katie agreed. "You're not like that, so you shouldn't dress that way."

My face grew hot. I understood "like that" to mean *slutty,* which in the world of Catholic school was a horrible insult that could brand your entire future.

Another time, in my early twenties, I was standing on the street with my mom and sister when a car full of guys drove by and beeped the horn and wolf-whistled. I recoiled. My sister preened. My mom laughed at our opposite reactions.

My sister loved the attention. I hated it. I just wanted to be able to stand on the street without men feeling like they had the right to ogle, cat-call, or comment on my body. And I felt a layer of shame about the attention.

Because the double bind I learned early on was this: *Your body is meant for men to enjoy. But if you're a "good girl," you should be ashamed when they do.*

Here's the truth, Jacqueline: Your body is meant for *you* to enjoy. And no matter its size or shape, you have no reason to be ashamed.

* * *

Let's fast-forward a decade or so to the time I was pregnant with you.

From the beginning, I carried you differently than I'd carried your brother. My tummy pooched out right away, as if to say, *We've done this before! We know the drill!*

So when I told Elijah's pediatrician that you were in my belly, he asked how far along I was.

"Eleven weeks," I said proudly. I was so excited.

The doctor raised his eyebrows. "Oh, wow," he said, and then paused. "Are you having twins?"

No, Jacqueline. I wasn't having twins.

The comments kept coming.

"You must be about to pop!" said a *stranger on the street,* when I was twenty-six weeks along.

"Wow! You've really grown since I saw you last!" one woman said.

"How many babies you got in there, anyway?" a man at church asked. That one stung my eyes with tears.

The truth is that I *felt* huge—big and ungainly and uncomfortable.

But when I got comments in the reverse, I didn't feel any better. I felt embarrassed and confused. One mom I know said: "You're so *skinny*! Are you sure you're eating enough?"

And then a woman commented on my baby bump to someone

while I was standing right in front of them: "She's hardly gained any weight at all. Bi-atch!"

I felt angry that so many people felt they had the right to comment on my body. And don't even get me started on the double standards. *You gained too much weight! You didn't gain enough!*

There is no winning, Jacqueline. The game is rigged.

* * *

It's like this: All my life, I've gotten memos about how my body should or shouldn't be. The memo that if I gained weight, I was undesirable. The memo that I shouldn't wear clothes that drew attention, because that meant I was "asking for it." The memo, always, that my body was too much or not enough.

I have so much rage, Jacqueline. And I have so much fear about bringing you up in a culture that programs women to believe that their bodies are shameful.

Because this is what I see: As women, we grow up thinking it's normal to hate ourselves. Normal for the men around us to feel entitled to comment on our bodies. Normal for our interior monologue to go: *You are ugly. Your stomach is disgusting.* Normal to size up other women: *Wow, she really gained a lot of weight. Ugh, she really let herself go.* But what I can see now, Jacqueline, is that while this hatred of our own bodies may be pervasive, it's not normal. And it's not right.

I want to build a different world.

A world where women collectively decide to disbelieve the lie that we must lose weight in order to be worthy. A world where women make friends with their own bodies. A world where we exchange all that self-hate for love, liberating a storm of energy to pour into creative, professional, and social justice pursuits.

This is the world I want to build with you.

* * *

Jacqueline, my love. Right now, your little body is driven to explore the world around you. You test the tactile sensation of paint between your fingers. You cram M&Ms into your mouth and squeal with delight as the sweetness bursts on your tongue. You climb everything; you dance to music, simply for the joy of movement.

You do not think in terms of how long you need to work out to burn off calories. You do not drag yourself out of bed exhausted at 5 a.m. to exercise so you can "maintain your weight."

As a result of growing you, carrying you, and pushing you out of my body—an act of heroism, a literal miracle—my body no longer fits the mold I've been programmed to believe is acceptable. My breasts sag. My belly pooches. My hips have love handles where they didn't before. And my upper arms now wave with me when I wave hello to our neighbors.

I have complicated feelings about this. Even though I know the measuring stick by which all women judge themselves (and each other) is just a tool of an oppressive patriarchal system.

Even though I know these things, I still feel shame.

And yet . . . here's the thing I keep coming back to: The writer Martha Beck once said, "Your children don't treat themselves the way you treated them. They treat themselves the way you treated yourself."

If I punish my body, that is what you will learn. If I stand in front of the mirror mentally castigating myself, that is what you will learn.

And so I begin. I begin committing myself to unwinding the patriarchy that's in my own brain, so I don't pass it down to you.

I begin making friends with my body again. I'm learning from you.

Go well, my beautiful daughter.

Love,
Mommy

Brooke Adams Law is an award-winning author and writing coach. Her debut novel, *Catchlight*, was named a Best Indie Book of 2020 by *Kirkus Reviews*. As a writing coach and head of a boutique publishing imprint, she leads first-time authors through a unique process that combines sophisticated storytelling technique with intuitive creativity. As the proud mama of Elijah and Jacqueline, she is committed to disrupting the culture of mom guilt.

The Anchor and the Seabird

SHANNON LEE

When I was a child, I used to dream I could breathe underwater. In the dream I knew how to stay submerged and recycle my air internally. It was natural. I would marvel at the sun through the mottled lens of the water while I happily acknowledged myself for my ability to sustain myself without surfacing. And the sun always seemed to be shining. In those dreams it was never night.

I was born with some peculiarities—a foot that turned in, fever-induced seizures, eyes that wandered outward, ears that ached and couldn't hear clearly. Could these have been vestiges of a former life lived underwater? I endured multiple surgeries and a surfeit of medications meant to amend my body of these ways, and I was starting to take shape as a terrestrial being at last when my father died unexpectedly, disappeared by some cruel land magic I did not understand. I was four, not quite formed, and the plane of my body, already inhospitable and tenuous, bent toward betrayal. Subconsciously it seemed only reasonable to retreat to the sea, but not as a former inhabitant. That life was lost to me now.

Rather, I made my body into an anchor, a land object abandoned to the abyss. Heavy.

There's not much tending required of an anchor. They are created to be swallowed whole by the deep, to remain silent and solid. Their destiny is to sink and leave depressions on the sea floor. This anchor would keep me centered in treacherous seas. It would eventually run me to the ground.

My father had been a real-life superhero. He was a warrior, a physical specimen, a teacher, and a diligent scholar. People were magnetized to him. He heralded the nature of water wherever he went. Had he, in fact, been some great fabled sea creature masquerading in human form? King Triton or Poseidon in disguise? Had this seaworthy demi-god coaxed me to trade in my mermaid tail for legs and then abandoned me to stumble around in a dry world with a burning sun?

In the wake of his absence, my water dreams turned to the vast, roiling ocean where it was always night. Creatures encircled me menacingly from below, large cumbersome animals that might come for me at any moment. I was tormented. Small. Afraid. Grief had locked away my childhood super powers, my sea magic lost like sunken treasure to the passing depths of time and growing older.

And so I lived in the sun, my life on full display: straight-A student, athlete, good girl, wife. A life imbued with superhero DNA that I used to bear the weight of the ocean. I longed to untether myself, to allow myself to rise, but I was afraid I would lose myself altogether. Would I fly? Or simply evaporate?

So I fed the anchor in me—eating food to feel full, being good to feel loved, consuming sweets to feel joy, staying quiet to remain invisible. There were many storms over the years that dragged me along the bottom, that dinged and dented me, and apathetic rust that threatened my integrity. But an anchor is unrelenting, and I was so wrapped up in the self-imposed mystery of being the water god's daughter that I began to fear it might be the only notable thing about me. I had forgotten that I too was of the sea.

As I grew, there were days when the sunshine did reach me, days when I was swept into shallower waters by a passing squall. Days when I could hear the song of the sea calling me, coaxing me to come to the surface and witness the sunlight dancing on the waves. There were days when I would daydream I was not an anchor at all, but a lotus flower reaching heroically through the mud, through the water, daring to let the sunlight touch my colored petals. What color would they be?

Many years passed and the days of my life along with them. When the day came to bring my daughter into the world, it was discovered that she had become fused to me, to my placenta, to her would-be place of nourishment. Had I unwittingly tethered her, too? Had I created a false center from enduring all the blows of "not being enough"?

The blows landed differently underwater. They were insidious that way. They were soft. They gathered and compounded. It was easy to miss the way they remade you into just another lost object consumed by mossy corrals and tiny sea creatures on the ocean floor. I had feared for so long that I might disappear that it had been happening for years.

My father, the water-god, hadn't intended to stun the inhabitants of Earth with his actions. He had intended to instruct me on how to shape shift. How to float on the currents while not relinquishing the sun. How to be not just one form, but all forms. Fluid. He hadn't sentenced me to life on Earth. I had done that.

So I took my anchor, this impressive, heavy, weighty thing I had manifested, and I bore it up from the ocean floor link by link because I am strong, and I showed it to my daughter. And I bade her watch as I examined it closely, cleaned it lovingly, and lavished it with gratitude for all it had done to serve me and keep me safe.

And then I began to dream again. But not the dream of an anchor wishing to be a lotus flower whose petals, though beautiful, were just a breath above the surface. No. I would need to dream higher than that. I would need to learn some new origami of the soul, some new way that reached further still.

So I worked diligently to remake myself every day. I forgave my past, drew my roots into myself so I would always have them with me, and untethered my future so that it was free to dream beyond the water's edge. Until one day, before our very eyes, we watched as what had once been an anchor now became a seabird.

And we could very clearly see that it could float effortlessly on the water, walk firmly on the shore, and fly freely in the sky, its feathers luminously catching the sun.

Shannon Lee is the author of *Be Water, My Friend*, which offers insight on how to use her father Bruce Lee's philosophies toward living a more fluid, peaceful, and fulfilling life. She is the CEO and owner of the Bruce Lee Family Companies and president of the Bruce Lee Foundation, and has spoken at TED, TEDx, and Creative Mornings. She lives in California with her daughter, Wren.

The Pandemic Taste Test

SUSAN SHAPIRO

I thought I had the perfect marriage—until the pandemic hit. While my husband and I were very lucky to be virus-free and able to work remotely, suddenly sharing breakfast, lunch, dinner, and snacks was disconcerting.

"Did you steal my Snickers?" he asked.

"Ate it at 3 a.m.," I confessed. "Why did you bring it home?"

"You stole it from *my* briefcase—in *my* den," he pointed out.

"We agreed to no candy or junk in the house," I repeated, referencing his promise to help my diet.

"Food insanity gets suspended in a global crisis!" he declared.

"Wrong! Disasters make everything worse. That's why the 'Corona 15' is trending," I yelled.

For a quarter century, my husband went to his office every day and returned late, so we often missed dinners together. Neither of us cooked well; we marked special occasions at our favorite seafood joint. As Manhattan workaholics who each held two jobs, I'd sometimes make us a meal of omelets or salmon, knowing my husband would indulge in fattening delicacies at work later. Our rule: What happens in the office stays in the office. He could consume whatever he wanted, just not in front of me, enhancing our independence. Only healthy cuisine filled our kitchen and cupboards.

But now, self-quarantine was breaking my careful routines and boundaries.

I wasn't tempted by his meatballs, pea soup, pickles, and smelly cheeses settling in our refrigerator. Yet during the lockdown—along with being a packrat who kept his baseball cards and bar mitzvah yarmulkes from childhood—my beloved became a food hoarder. From his short walks, mail runs, and ordering in, he brought home dumplings, noodle concoctions, matzo ball soup, peanut butter, tuna salad, half pounds of cold cuts, rolls, pita— enough to feed a family of twelve in a bunker for months. But we were only two, and one of us struggled to stem a lifetime of disordered eating with the mandate: "Out of sight, out of mind."

Was this the kind of offense that could cause a corona-divorce?

"No crackers," I snapped one day as he unpacked his latest bounty. "I can't do bread products."

"So Triscuits are your gateway drug?" he quipped.

He didn't get that my food addiction wasn't cute. It could make me spiral out of control, screwing up my body, head, and our relationship.

When I threatened to toss the box, he screamed, "Are you nuts? People are starving in this country!"

"So leave some food on the shelves for them!" I countered, reminding him that I'd donated to food banks and funds to feed essential workers, along with buying a bunch of my students' groceries.

Since my husband was over sixty with medical issues, I soon insisted on gathering our grub by myself. Feeling wildly protective and petrified of losing him, I was also determined to control the influx of big bags into our little kitchen.

He started emailing me lists of provocative provisions. When I accidentally forgot his toasted bagel and ice cream, he sneered, "Freud says there's no such thing as a coincidence."

"Why do I have to buy crap I don't want to see that's gonna screw me up?" I countered. "Order it in yourself."

When I found half a bag of chocolate-covered pretzels in his closet, I polished it off and then confessed.

"You know, your mom sent me those LAST YEAR," he defended. "I have one a month."

Bad enough my Jewish mother sent him secret treats. Worse, I'd unwittingly wed someone who could eat just one chocolate-covered pretzel monthly. We were clearly incompatible.

I flashed back to our first blind date, when he offered me shrimp tempura on chopsticks. A twenty-nine-year-old, five-foot-seven, 123-pound gym rat, I shook my head.

The cute forty-year-old six-foot-four schlep, carrying an extra sixty pounds, reminded me of my beloved Michigan brothers. Moving east for grad school, I'd walked miles daily, proud to be the most in-shape Shapiro. I hadn't yet realized that drinking, smoking, and toking suppressed my appetite.

Within days of exchanging vows, my husband said, "You have to quit cigarettes, alcohol, and partying."

Could your mate demand that you stop being self-destructive? I wanted to leave. But I'd just said "I do" in front of the rabbi, judge, friends, and relatives. I'd given up my old apartment. Plus—I loved him.

"If you'd said that while we dated, I wouldn't have married you," I told him.

"That's why I waited," he admitted.

After addiction therapy to stop smoking, drinking, and all drugs, my obsessions gravitated toward food—the hardest substance to conquer because you couldn't just quit. Ceasing entire categories like candy and ice cream was easier than moderation for me. Yet my husband maintained his greasy fried fetish and refused to exercise.

"If I have to stop my bad habits, so do you," I decided.

He shocked me by quitting beer and pizza. Within weeks he modeled old Levi's that hadn't fit for years. Within months, he showed off hideous plaid college blazers he could wear again.

Down sixty pounds, he'd constantly ask, "Am I still looking thin?"

He was, while consuming twice what I did. Then I tore two ligaments in my back and had knee surgery for a torn meniscus, unable to do anything aerobic right around menopause. He'd lost weight and I found it; I felt like Jack Sprat and his wife. When his wedding ring loosened around his slimmer finger, I worried.

"Susan, if I ever cheat on you, it will be with pizza," he reassured me.

Now nearly a year into the global health crisis, nervously watching updates on TV, mourning friends who died, and reading a colleague's harrowing account of taking care of her deathly ill spouse who could no longer eat, I see how blessed we were to (metaphorically) break bread daily, grateful we could still feed each other.

"What do you want for breakfast, honey?" I asked him this morning, before rushing out to get his favorite whitefish, meatballs, matzo ball soup, rice cakes, and Haribo ginger-lemon candies. I vowed self-control, respect, staying out of his space. When that faltered, we found a solution to maintain the mystery. Last night, putting on a mask and plastic gloves, he said, "I'm picking up my prescription downstairs." It was a code, I gathered, for, "I'll finish my Snickers in the elevator."

Susan Shapiro is the bestselling author of thirteen books her family hates, like *Unhooked, Five Men Who Broke My Heart, Lighting Up,* her inspiring publishing guide *The Byline Bible,* and her new memoir *The Forgiveness Tour.* She's a longtime Manhattan writing professor who now teaches her popular Instant Gratification Takes Too Long classes and seminars online.

ACKNOWLEDGMENTS

The acknowledgments section for my previous anthology was so long that when my aunt read it, she forwarded it to some friends and said, "I think she thanked everyone but her doorman." I wrote back and said, "Shoot! I forgot to thank my doorman." So, Steve and Eric, this one's for you.

This time I'll keep it short(er) and sweet.

1. The biggest thank you in the world to the authors who contributed to this collection. I am honored you took the time to share your innermost thoughts in such beautiful ways. Truly.
2. Thank you to Carolyn Murnick, the real editor of this anthology. (I think my role should be described as "curator.") She worked tirelessly to perfect the essays and make them all even stronger. Thanks also to Kera Bolonik for the copyediting.
3. A huge thanks to the team at Skyhorse Publishing, especially Tony Lyons, Mark Gompertz, and Caroline Russomanno.
4. Thanks to my literary agent Joe Veltre at Gersh who took a chance on me. We've now sold five books together in fourteen months and we're just getting started. (Knock wood.)
5. Thanks to my own team and everyone I work with for helping with this project and everything else that moms don't have time to do. Chelsea Grogan, Nina Vargas, Laura Rossi, Jordan Blumetti, Emily Sharp, Tracey Cox, Sherri Lynn Puzey, Genevieve McCormack, Kathy Salem, Trina Cianfrone, Bobby

Grossman, Jackie Eckhouse, Sara Grambusch, Steven Ejbick, Ryan MacNeill, and everyone who has helped me do anything ever. Seriously.

6. Thanks to all the authors and guests who have come on my podcasts. I've truly loved our conversations. And thanks to all the sponsors!
7. Thanks to the many amazing authors who blurbed this book including Christina Baker Kline, Jane L. Rosen, Billie Lourd, Annabelle Gurwitch, Stephanie Thornton Plymale, Jo Piazza, and Meaghan B. Murphy.
8. Thanks to all the media superstars that have featured me or my previous anthology in the press and will hopefully cover this book, too (!!!), plus the many, many other amazing creatives who have had me on their podcasts, radio shows, blogs, book groups, or did Instagram Lives with me.
9. Thanks to all the bookstores and organizations who hosted events for me last time like BookHampton, Parnassus Books, Anderson's Bookshops, BookPeople, the Temple Emanuel Streicker Center, the North Castle Public Library, the JCC, UJA, the Center for Fiction, CMEE, and many more.
10. Thanks to all my amazing girlfriends who I've barely seen this year. I miss you.
11. Thanks to my family and extended family for absolutely everything. My mom and Howard, my dad and Christine, my brother Teddy and Ellen plus their three amazing kids, my father-in-law Bernard and step-mother-in-law, Miriam, my sister-in-law Stefanie, Aunt Lizzie, my aunts and uncles, and all my cousins.
12. To my kids. (I'm making the "I love you" sign.) Thanks for letting me pursue my dreams of writing books and doing podcasts. And thanks for spending so much time on your iPads this pandemic when I was busy doing it all; you guys played Roblox so much that the company ended up going public. I bought one

share for each of you. You're welcome. In all seriousness, the four of you are so important to me that a simple paragraph in the back of a book would never cut it. You're more important than a paragraph, a page, or any book on earth. To me, you are the entire planet. The be all and end all. But you already know that.

13. To my four Moms Don't Have Time To Fellows who I know will make a difference in the world (no pressure): Meghan Riordan Jarvis, Rev. Lydia Sohn, Cristina Alesci, and Mireya D'Angelo, plus Leigh Newman and Carolyn Murnick for the editing.
14. Thanks to my Instagram followers. I love you guys! Your likes and comments keep me going on the darkest days. (Follow me on social! @zibbyowens on Instagram. That'll take you everywhere you need to go!)
15. Thanks to all the readers of my last anthology and of all my essays. It means so much to me to know you're reading my thoughts and not throwing the books or articles in the trash in disgust. (And that if you are doing that, you've chosen not to tell me. So thank you.)
16. Thanks to all my podcast listeners! I appreciate every single download!!! Keep at it. (Please?!?!?)
17. Thanks to all the book club members in Zibby's Virtual Book Club!
18. Thanks to all the members of my "village" who pitch in to help with kids, home, and everything else that keeps me sane and allows me to be productive in my professional life.
19. Finally, thanks to Kyle for kissing me that first day at the beach, even though I was trying to scare you away. You said then that you were "all in" and you've been by my side ever since. I don't deserve you. I wouldn't even be "Zibby Owens" without you. Thanks for making all of this happen. But I would've been happy just getting to spend KZ Time with you.

How was that? Better?!

ABOUT THE EDITOR

Zibby Owens is the CEO of Moms Don't Have Time To, a media company she founded featuring podcasts, publications, and communities.

Zibby hosts the award-winning podcast *Moms Don't Have Time to Read Books* and *Moms Don't Have Time to Lose Weight*. She is the author/editor of the anthology *Moms Don't Have Time To: A Quarantine Anthology*, all proceeds of which go to the Susan Felice Owens Program for Covid-19 Vaccine Research in honor of her late mother-in-law.

She is the editor in chief of *Moms Don't Have Time to Write*, a Medium Publication, and founder of The Zibby Awards, celebrating the overlooked parts of books. She also founded the Moms Don't Have Time To Fellowship.

Named "NYC's Top Book-fluencer" by *Vulture* and on Oprah's list of top podcasts two years in a row, Zibby is a frequent contributor to *Good Morning America*, the *Washington Post*, *Good Day LA*, and other media outlets. She has two children's books forthcoming from Flamingo, a Penguin Random House imprint.

Zibby currently lives in New York with her husband, Kyle Owens of Morning Moon Productions, and her four children ages six to thirteen. She always has a book nearby. Follow her on Instagram @zibbyowens.